Between Two Cultures

PETER LANG
New York • Washington, D.C./Baltimore • Bern
Frankfurt am Main • Berlin • Brussels • Vienna • Oxford

Mitra Das

Between Two Cultures

The Case of Cambodian Women in America

PETER LANG
New York • Washington, D.C./Baltimore • Bern
Frankfurt am Main • Berlin • Brussels • Vienna • Oxford

Library of Congress Cataloging-in-Publication Data
Das, Mitra.
Between two cultures: the case of Cambodian women in America / Mitra Das.
p. cm.
Includes bibliographical references.
1. Cambodian Americans. 2. Women immigrants—
United States—History. I. Title.
E184.K45D37   305.48'89593073—dc22   2006023631
ISBN-13: 978-0-8204-7493-9
ISBN-10: 0-8204-7493-2

Bibliographic information published by **Die Deutsche Nationalbibliothek**.
Die Deutsche Nationalbibliothek lists this publication in the "Deutsche
Nationalbibliografie"; detailed bibliographic data are available
on the Internet at http://dnb.d-nb.de/.

Cover design by Sophie Boorsch Appel

The paper in this book meets the guidelines for permanence and durability
of the Committee on Production Guidelines for Book Longevity
of the Council of Library Resources.

© 2007, 2015 Peter Lang Publishing, Inc., New York
29 Broadway, 18th floor, New York, NY 10006
www.peterlang.com

All rights reserved.
Reprint or reproduction, even partially, in all forms such as microfilm,
xerography, microfiche, microcard, and offset strictly prohibited.

Printed in the United States

In appreciation and support for all those who suffered and survived the tragedies in their homelands and shared their life stories with me

Contents

Preface	ix
One: Coming to America	1
Two: Origins of the Journey: Where They Came from and Why?	21
Three: All America City	39
Four: A New Beginning: Challenges and Opportunities	55
Five: From Tradition to Modern: Family Changes Among Cambodian Women	75
Six: Toward Empowerment: Community Institution Building	93
Seven: Conclusion	113
Notes	123
Illustrations	133

Preface

This is a study of Cambodian women in Lowell, Massachusetts. I am an immigrant myself and have the benefit of experiencing first hand what it is to be so. This gives me a comparative perspective. This study is based on the information provided by the women I interviewed and the journeys they have made as they settled in Lowell following the events in their homeland in which they were unwittingly caught. This information is often presented as personal anecdotes the way I received it. The size of the Cambodian community has been its greatest strength. It is this numerical strength that has been a channel for voices to be heard such that programs of empowerment through a variety of organizations could be formulated. Of course, this size has also created problems that have taxed the system, as the pages of the book will reveal. When I started this study, there was little information available about this group. In fact, I was encouraged to write about the experiences and the agony this group had gone through en route to their settlement in this country by Sithra Chan, the first Cambodian woman I met. I am grateful to her.

This project has been made possible because of the help I have received from a variety of sources both within and outside the university community. The Healy Grant that I received from the University of Massachusetts Lowell was the first seed. that helped me with interviews of the people who are part of this study. I am especially thankful to Phala Chea and Nicole Witherbee, who accompanied me on some of the interview sessions. Phala interpreted and translated interviews where the women had no or very little knowledge of English. Thanks are also due to Kristin Esterberg who commented on the prospectus for this study, Charles Carroll who provided resources to complete this project, and Susan Thomson who commented on my work and gave me information of others involved in this community. James Higgins, Joan Ross, and Tim Chan Thou very graciously allowed me to use their photographs that depict some of the themes discussed in the book. I am grateful to all of them. Chanda and Marina Moul and Sokha Sorn also provided photos for use for this book. I thank them for sharing them with me. I also wish to acknowledge the help of Rani Bose, Arun Paul, and Abhijit Das in completing the maps and diagrams from the U.S. Census and other sources that are included in this book. There are others also—students, colleagues, and citizens of the state—who directed me to information or was its source. I thank them one and all, even though I may not be able to cite each of them by name.

This is not a study of *all* the issues out there that confront this community. It is a small piece of the big and ongoing process. I have attempted to give a comprehensive and a holistic picture of this group, comparing it to other groups wherever relevant. I have attempted to accurately present the information as it was presented to me. The writing, however, is entirely mine. So are its shortcomings.

Lowell, MA
June 2006

CHAPTER ONE

Coming to America

Introduction

I came to the United States at a historical time when the laws permitting immigration to this country had recently changed, and I was a beneficiary of these changes. I am an immigrant to this country and have experienced first hand what being an immigrant to this country entails. I have also read of experiences of other immigrant groups of different ethnic backgrounds. Therefore, writing about immigrant experiences of people who have settled in the United States is challenging and gratifying at the same time. Many scholars have written about the history and problems of immigrants in America. This is a field of study that has received attention from social scientists and politicians alike. It is also a phenomenon that is associated with a lot of beliefs, some of which are popularly held but not necessarily corroborated by facts.[1] As new émigrés are admitted to this country and become noticeable, their visibility evokes a lot of debate and discourse about the desirability of having people of different ethnicities in society and their effects and contributions to this society. This book attempts to examine and understand one such group— namely Cambodians— who came as refugees to this country and have attempted to resettle in a city historically known for its ethnic and immigrant history.

The Debate and the Reality

After a lapse of more than five decades, the United States began to admit large numbers of immigrants from countries of the world that had been excluded from immigration to this land due to their national origin. As diverse groups of people started entering in large numbers, questions were raised about whether it was good or bad for the country and whether this flow should be curtailed to keep the culture of the United States intact. The debate about admitting newcomers from 'different shores' to this country has evoked strong emotions depending upon the prevailing economy and political culture of the times. Both the proponents and opponents of immigration have argued about the benefits and disadvantages, respectively, of allowing foreigners to come and settle in this country. A poll in the *Time* magazine in the fall of 1993 reported an increasing numbers of the sampled people—approximately 75%—opted for strict limiting of immigration compared to a quarter that opined to keep the doors to immigration open.[2] More recently, in the 2004 presidential election, the issue picked up momentum with groups of people around the border states in the Southwest protesting against the admission of workers as cheap labor coming from across the border in Mexico. And this debate—about admitting aliens—is not a new one, although the issues around which it has polarized have changed with time. It dates back to the time that United States first started allowing immigrants to come to this country. Anti-immigrant feelings and actions by those already settled in this country against an incoming group have been a part of our history. Notwithstanding all this, the fact remains that immigration and immigrants have left an indelible mark in the history and culture of American society since the time the first immigrants crossed into America some 30,000 years ago.[3] A critical scrutiny of American culture is likely to reveal its foreign origins. The ancestors of everyone who lives in the United States originally came from somewhere else. As they came and settled here, they also brought with them aspects of their cultures. With passage of time these became accepted as part of American mainstream society. In actuality, one can safely state that it is difficult to think about American history and culture without immigrants.[4] And the immigrant story continues as new groups of people from other parts of the world seek entry into this country in the hope of achieving a better life than was available in their native homelands. American immigration is comparable to movements of waves in an ocean. It is unending. As one wave recedes, another takes its place.

The United States takes in more immigrants (and refugees) than all other countries of the world.[5] As a nation, it is ethnically more diverse compared to what it was in the middle of the twentieth century. Terms such as *diversity* and *pluralism* are part of the current politically correct vocabulary. America is a nation of immigrants. People from around the world have come to its shores seeking opportunities for a new and better life. Yet the newcomers to this land have not always been welcomed with open arms. They have been admitted but have been left more or less on their own to fend for themselves. This was true in the past. It is also generally true today, although some legislation enacted in the last two decades of the twentieth century has provided social welfare aid to some newcomers depending on their legal status of entry.

The United States is heralded as a nation of immigrants, but is also a country that abhors immigration. These opposing ideas continue to dot our cultural landscape. In the nineteenth century some of the best and brightest minds in the United States were opposed to immigration of any people except White Anglo-Saxon Protestants (WASP). They were convinced of the natural superiority of the Anglo-Saxon people and attempted to curb the immigration of people (including Europeans) who did not fall under this ethnic category.[6] Although the gates of America were later opened to other Europeans besides Anglo-Saxon Protestants, hostility to new immigrants persisted. Even ethnic groups who now hold the reigns of power were not spared differential treatment when they first arrived as immigrants to this country. The Irish, who entered this country in large numbers in the nineteenth century after the potato famine in Ireland provide a case in point. As new immigrants, they were not immune from hostility. In the burgeoning industrial town of Lowell, Massachusetts, where many Irish came in search of work, signs were posted outside many stores that read "Irish need not apply." This was an indication of the hatred and contempt with which they were treated. Initially, the Irish came in as canal diggers, their labor necessary for the economy of the region, but they were not welcome as residents in Lowell. They lived segregated lives, in squalor in a parcel of land known as the Acre given to them for domicile. This was the first slum in Lowell.[7]

Despite the hatred and prejudice the Irish encountered, they were later hired in the textile factories of Lowell, to replace the exodus of the native-born Americans who began leaving the factories due to declining wages and deteriorating working conditions. The Irish were only too glad to have found jobs and initially worked and lived under miserable conditions and faced many hardships. Even their whiteness did not exempt them from discrimination. They had to prove that they were fit to be American. The process of becoming white and becoming American were interconnected.[8] However, in due time they were able to overcome many of the social handicaps that afflicted them and were able to create institutions such as their own churches that helped them live the life that they had known back at home. As they moved up and began accessing positions of power and influence in the town government, established and prospered in businesses they opened, they left their former positions in the factories to other immigrant groups who came after them in search of work and a better life.

The same process has been repeated over time for other European immigrants into Lowell who came after them. More recently newcomers of color who have settled into Lowell have faced situations of hostility and have been blamed for some of the city's problems. A report of the Massachusetts Attorney General's Civil Rights division in 1983 noted the numbers of racially motivated assaults against the Southeast Asian refugees.[9] The death of a 13-year-old Cambodian youth in Lowell due to drowning was the result of racial attack by a white teenager who pushed him into the river. Some of the women I interviewed for this study confided in me the kind of racial indignities they had to put up with at work due to their ethnic origin. Two women who worked at the same place reported the differential treatment they received compared to white American women who were their colleagues. One woman reported that her boss would throw things at her rather than give them to her. Another woman did not want to talk about racism on the premises lest someone hear her. Still others have reported of other forms of prejudicial treatments encountered by them. One woman stated that when she bought a new car, it was assumed that she was able to do it because of the welfare payments she received. That she had worked hard to save the money to buy it was discounted. She noted that when she achieved material success (in the form of an automobile or the house she bought) her white neighbors were envious of her success. Another person noted, "Sometimes Americans are jealous when we buy a new car."[10] This is in tune with the fact that people of color have to work harder (than members of the dominant majority) to achieve their goals and when they do so, their success is attributed to supports they receive from the government. I have heard some Asian friends in very responsible positions tell me of their encounters of latent prejudice from their white colleagues who assumed that they got their positions not due to their merit but because of affirmative action. I have heard many students in my classes complain of how white people get by passed by minority candidates for advertised positions in civil service due to affirmative action despite their lower scores in the written exams. Of course, they are never able to substantiate these allegations, which, if true would be reflected in the official numbers of hires by race and ethnicity in a given department.

Despite the hostility, immigrants have played a crucial role in the development of American society. For example, whenever there has been a shortage of labor in American industries, immigrants have been recruited to fill the gap. This is an occurrence that dates back to a time when the United States was developing into an industrial society. The U.S. government admitted people into the country, allowing them to work for employers that needed them. Alternatively, the lure of job openings and a prospect of a better life have attracted prospective job seekers to the doors of potential employers. This has happened from the nineteenth century to present times. When the newcomers are seen as competitors by the people settled before them, a campaign has often been mounted against them. In the nineteenth and the twentieth centuries there have been instances of anti-immigration agitation both for cultural and economic reasons. Sometimes the quality of their cultural stock was suspect. At other times they were seen as economically displacing the work force. This dual aspect of U.S.immigrant history has recurred time and again. New immigrant groups have often been met with resistance and hostility from those before them. Yet that has not discouraged people from different walks of life and different regions of the world to come to this "land of opportunity." Thousands of people worldwide lacking opportunities of a hopeful future in their homeland have dreamed of coming to this region of seemingly infinite resources where they could start afresh and create better lives for themselves and their families. In contemporary times one need only to look at the long lines of people waiting for visa or entry permits outside U.S. consulate offices or Embassies in some major cities of the most populous countries of the world. In places such as Mumbai (Bombay), India, I have seen long lines of potential immigrants, stretching approximately a quarter mile onto the main street from the consulate office. People wait patiently on the pavement to get into the consulate office for an interview that would allow them to get the much-coveted visa that would enable them to come to this country. Yet a third route of entry has been for people who have come as refugees to this country or sought political asylum due to grave danger to their lives in their country of origin.[11]

From the Old to the New Immigrants

For more than a century, from 1820 to 1920 when the U.S. population grew from 10 million to 100 million, 90% of all immigrants were Europeans. In fact the words European and immigrant were used interchangeably by some.[12] Africans were forcibly brought to this country as slave labor, and out of the equation of immigration. If one examines the statistical census data of immigration between the period of 1820 to 1960, it is evident that during this time period the immigrants principally came from regions of Europe.[13] Very few people came from countries other than Europe. The Asians (Chinese) were admitted in the middle of the nineteenth century as cheap labor for mining and railway construction. Initially, the Chinese were received with a lot of fanfare and curiosity. However, when their numbers began to increase, this admiration was replaced with hostility and resentment, especially when the Chinese were seen as economic competitors and cultural contaminators of the American way of life. There was a frenzy of anti-Chinese sentiment, and some areas were the venue of severe violent incidents against them. Federal legislation was passed to severely limit and restrict Chinese immigration, and this was accomplished with the Chinese Exclusion Act of 1892. From the end of the nineteenth century the numbers of Chinese entering the country were severely restricted. Thus essentially people of European descent came as immigrants in the early phase of U.S immigrant history and accounted for the majority of the immigrants coming to the United States.

The Eurocentric immigration pattern continued for the first six decades of the twentieth century. As late as the 1950s Europeans represented more than half of all the immigrants to this country. This began to change from the middle of the twentieth century. The ethnic pool became increasingly diverse as peoples from regions of the world hitherto barred from entry were legally allowed immigration to this country. The restrictions on immigration based on national origin or ethnicity instituted earlier in response to fears of social contamination were lifted with the enactment of new immigration laws in 1965. This Immigration and Naturalization Act came into full affect in 1968. It abolished Asiatic exclusion and permitted people to legally enter the country on the basis of occupational skills needed for the market, family reunification, and fear of political and religious persecution.[14] With the enactment of this legislation, the numbers of immigrants in the United States from parts of the world other than Western Europe and Canada increased significantly. The Immigration Act of 1965 facilitated immigration of peoples from various countries of Asia so that the Asian American population doubled in the 1970s and again during the 1980s. In 1970 there were less than 1.5 million Asian Americans in the United States. By 1990 their numbers had grown to 7.3 million. In 2000 there were 11.9 million Asians, constituting 4.2% of the U.S. population.[15] Asian Americans are the fastest growing minority in the nation. The influx of Asian people[16] into the ethnic mix has had differential impact on groups depending on a complex array of factors. These include both the prevailing conditions of the host society as well as the characteristics of the émigré population.

The Asian Immigrants

The wave of Asian immigrants into the United States following the changes in the immigration laws consisted basically of two categories of people. The first were self-selected. People in this group came voluntarily, in pursuit of opportunities and life chances perceived as unavailable or difficult to attain in their homelands. The doctor or the engineer from places such as India, Taiwan, or Korea came to the United States not to escape the poverty of their homelands, but to eke out a new and better professional life and standard of living envisioned not possible in their country of origin. Similarly, labor migrants both legal and illegal who came as workers in search of jobs in industries that experienced a deficit in labor supply are also part of the same category. The second group of people came to this country out of sheer necessity. They were forced to leave their homes and countries because of political persecution or the wars raging in their homelands. These included the waves of refugees who came to this country in the decade of the 1970s following the withdrawal of U.S. troops from Southeast Asia.

The war in Southeast Asia (in which the United States was involved) saw a mass exodus of people from such countries as Cambodia, Vietnam, and Laos. The Southeast Asian refugees to this country came in three waves.[17] The first wave largely included the Vietnamese; very few Cambodians arrived at this time. Their numbers increased in the second migratory wave, which also included people from Vietnam and Laos. For the first time, as many as 10,000 Cambodians may have arrived in the United States as part of the Southeast Asian refugees coming to the United States. The third wave of refugee migration contained the largest numbers of Cambodian refugees. This wave of refugees principally consisted of people of disadvantaged class positions, with very little school education and single-parent (female) families with young children. Some of the people fleeing their wartorn homeland came to the United States when that government agreed to admit them as refugees. (Other countries that took Southeast Asian refugees were France and Australia.) People fleeing persecution had sought and gotten political asylum in the United States in the past. But no separate policy existed to admit refugees until the Refugee Act of 1980. The Refugee Act of 1980 addressed this inadequacy. Between April 1975 and September 1984, 711,000 refugees of Asian origin were admitted to the United States. By 1990, these refugees, when added to Asians in the U.S., population, represented more than one out of every seven Asian Americans.[18] These are the most recent Asian Americans to come to this country. And though they may share some cultural characteristics with other Asian immigrants before them, their experience of settling in the United States is different from other Asian counterparts by virtue of the conditions that brought them to this country. Unlike other Asian Americans, the Southeast Asians came mainly as refugees and not as immigrants thus contributing to the diversity of incorporation of Asian Americans. The U.S. immigration experience therefore unmistakably also involves the experiences of these Southeast Asian refugee migrants, a group that came under very different circumstances at a time when the U.S. ethnic mix was becoming very diverse. Their incorporation therefore is also a part of the general drama of the 'immigrant experience' in America and needs to be examined.

Asian American residents are noted as having an impact on this country far beyond what their numbers warrant.[19] In the Silicon Valley of California, the Mecca of high tech companies, a news source had reported 30 percent of its high-tech start-up companies were headed by people of Asian origin. The advantage that the United States gets from the contribution of its immigrants is even acknowledged by its president when he stated, "Our technology advantage rests on the contributions of immigrants in places like India or China. . . ."[20] In many aspects of American life, Asian accomplishment has been remarkably visible. Immigrants from many Asian countries top the list of people in the category of highest proportion of college-educated groups in the United States.[21] A news article some years ago reported that many nationally known top-ranking colleges were attempting to restrict admission of Asian students in an effort to make their numbers proportionate to their presence in the population at large. Due to publicity of such achievements, the thesis of *model minority* has gained momentum. But this does not imply that all Asian Americans have an easy time in the United States. First of all, Asian Americans are not a homogenous group. Second, there are many factors that affect the experiences of newcomers to this country.[22] Although shared common backgrounds of ethnic groups may account for some similarities in their experiences, distinct historical and social conditions of their lives nevertheless are likely to affect the issues they confront as they engage in the process of resettlement. According to one report, similarity in professional skills and backgrounds may be more powerful than ethnic background in accounting for similar immigrant experience.[23] On the other hand, ethnicity may have an overriding influence among people struggling to make it in America where the presence of strong ethnic ties may be used as a support mechanism to overcome the disadvantages that absence of professional skills entail. Later on we will see how the numerical strength of the Cambodians in Lowell has been utilized to get grants from the government for addressing some of the issues confronted by the community as it engaged in the process of resettlement.

Cambodians, the Asian newcomers from Southeast Asia, are from "different shores" and ethnically and culturally distinct from immigrants of European descent who constituted the bulk of immigrant to this country until the 1950s. They are also distinct from the other Asian immigrants who came before them following the changes in immigration laws of 1965, since they generally entered this country as refugees after the 1980 legislation to facilitate their entry. They are therefore of special interest for studying the issues of adaptation and assimilation. On the one hand, they provide an opportunity to examine the recent immigrant experience of newcomers to this land while it is happening. On the other hand, their distinctiveness is an asset for comparing the problems and benefits, similarities and differences involved in the process of adaptation and incorporation in U.S. society. It is therefore not surprising that it is a group much written about.

The city of Lowell, because of its large concentration of South Asian refugees, provides a natural lab to study the issues of adaptation encountered by immigrants in general and Southeast Asians in particular. The Cambodian diaspora in Lowell is the second largest in the United States— according to some estimates, almost a fourth of its population is Cambodian. Historically, Lowell is known for being an immigrant city. Ever since its inception in 1824 it has provided refuge to diverse peoples from different parts of the world that came to it looking for work and made it their home.

Perspective and Factors in Adaptation: Some Examples

The immigrant experience of newcomers who join the ranks of those before them is a complex one. Scholars have noted both the uprooting experience as well as the adaptive influences that immigrant institutions and resources make possible. The dominant model in the social sciences has posited the idea that in due time immigrants pick up traits that are in conformity with the mainstream/dominant groups in society and shed some of their ethnic peculiarities. In other words, they become Americanized.[24] This is the idea that is associated with the *assimilation model* that has dominated immigrant scholarship.

This theory, with its emphasis on absorption of Anglo-Saxon core culture has recently been challenged because of its neglect of non-European immigrant groups whose immigrant experience is at variance with the generation of white immigrants who comfortably fit in with this model. Yet others have pointed that the process of adaptation is not unilinear or uniform and is affected by multiple factors having to do with historical and other developments. One can safely state that in a developing American industrial economy the factors affecting process of assimilation were likely to be different from the present time where the structural basis of the economy has undergone radical shifts and is more tied to the forces of the global market. It is this that makes the process of adaptation today even more complex.

The process of social adaptation of newcomers, whether they come in as immigrants or refugees, thus is complex and multifaceted and varies with historical circumstances. Many factors influence this process. Some examples are cited here to show this variability. At the very outset there is the issue of economic survival. The historical time, the economy, the governmental policies in place, family composition and structure, age, and the skills one possesses are but a few of the factors that influence this process of adaptation. For example, the Mexican Americans and Puerto Ricans, two Latino groups that came to Chicago to seek economic opportunities, lagged behind ethnic groups of Europeans descent that came before them. The Mexican Americans came to Chicago during World War I to fill the labor needs of the industries such as steel and railways facing disputes and strikes. Although promised permanent employment, they were fired once the labor disputes were settled.[25] Despite their contributions to the labor market, they were particularly vulnerable to racial discrimination. The Puerto Ricans, on the other hand, came at a time when major structural changes were reducing the importance of manufacturing as a major provider of new jobs. However, both these groups developed a common political consciousness to seek redress for their conditions with the placement of the Affirmative Action Policy following the Civil Rights Act of 1964 that empowered them. In mobilizing along ethnic lines, they were able to wield power and get the economic elites of the city to address their needs.

The French Canadians who migrated to Lowell, Massachusetts, from the middle to the late nineteenth century illustrate the importance of age and family structure in the process of economic survival. The French Canadians came to Lowell at a time when it was a developing industrial economy in need of labor to fill the jobs required in the factory system. The French Canadians who came after the Irish were able to find jobs in the textile mills of Lowell. Life and living were difficult and tough. Yet some were able to use family resources and values as an adaptive tool of adjustment.[26] The presence of many children of working age in the family was economically advantageous as their labor was utilized to increase family income and the familial standard of living. Indeed, families with children of working age were economically better off compared to those families whose children were too young to work.[27] The examples cited thus far indicate the importance of economic survival and how the resources at the disposal of the immigrant communities can be harnessed towards economic empowerment.

Aside from the problems of economic survival, there are also issues of social and cultural adaptation that confront an incoming group. The road to settlement entails accommodation to existing institutions and structures. One has to learn the way things are done here if one is to go about the business of living in this country so that one is not in violation of existing rules of civic behavior. "Newcomers must learn what is appropriate and what is not in *this* culture"[28] if they are to be respected by the dominant majority. In a published piece entitled "Culture and Law"[29] it was reported that housing conditions in a Lowell tenement housing complex on Branch Street inspected by building inspectors was truly shocking. The shock came from the building code and health violations that existed in the apartment. There was evidence of live and freshly butchered animals, meats hanging in the kitchen, and piles of trash stacked behind the building. This underscores the importance of educating newcomers in urban lifestyles for both health and intergroup harmonious relationships. This particular instance is cited here to point out that cultural practices are contextual. In the agrarian life lived in villages of Cambodia, it may have been usual and normal to kill the animals in the family yard just before they were prepared for the family meal. But in an apartment dwelling in an urban environment such activities can be health hazards. Also, because of housing shortage many families lived in very crowded situations where as many as eight people were living in a single bedroom apartment.

The importance of acting according to the existing and prevailing norms of the society can also be illustrated by a very different situation. I have been told that many Cambodian families have arranged marriages of their daughters according to traditional cultural customs. However, because these are not legally recognized by the state, the partners in question are not entitled to the rights and privileges that marriage grants. (This issue is discussed in a later chapter.) This again points to the importance of knowing the rules of the country of domicile for successful adaptation and integration.

Living in a society and culture that is distinctly different from one's homeland also heightens one's own cultural identity encouraging people to retain their cultural ways. Immigrants have often been torn between "old loyalties and new realities."[30] Nowhere is this better seen than when the children of migrants come of age and are interested in "being American." This brings the clash between the parents' and their children's generations. History is replete with examples of different ethnic groups attempting to maintain their cultural ways after coming to America. Indeed, coming to America transforms immigrants into ethnics. Exposure to American society brings out their national identities.[31] If one looks at the ethnic map of the United States, there are distinct ethnic settlement patterns discernible across the country, where people of different ethnic heritages are concentrated. The West Coast and the East Coast have concentrations of Southeast Asians. Orange County in Los Angeles is the home to the largest Vietnamese community outside of Vietnam, just as Long Beach in Los Angeles in the home to the largest Cambodian community. Residential concentration of people by ethnicity brings with it its particular cultural flavor that distinguishes one group from another. The areas where Chinese are concentrated are distinct from areas dominated by the Indians, just as the areas principally inhabited by the Southeast Asians in parts of Massachusetts are distinguished by cultural markers that are the badge of their identity. One of the distinguishing marks of ethnic neighborhoods consists of the food shops that spring up catering to the ethnic palates of its inhabitants. These are later followed by other kinds of activities including ethnic shops providing different goods and services and the establishment of churches and temples to service its believers. As one drives down Branch Street in Lowell, Massachusetts, one is likely to see a number of shops, grocery stores, restaurants, and jewelry stores owned by Cambodian shop owners that service the needs of the community members.

One can safely state that the problems encountered by the first generation of immigrants are different than those encountered by subsequent generations. The first to arrive are pioneers, embarking upon journeys that are unknown. The challenges they face—of physical survival to those of cultural adaptation—are unprecedented. I arrived in this country a little over three decades ago. Soon after arrival, my husband and I had to first find affordable housing and get settled so that we could carry on with our educational programs for which we had originally come. After completing my graduate studies, I found a job, raised a family, and was able to achieve a comfortable lifestyle. But in raising a family in the United States. I encountered many cultural issues that were distinctly "American." As a working woman I had to cope with the problems of child-care that many of my counterparts around the world face. But my problem was also cultural. While working full time, I was expected to be a traditional housewife and a daughter-in-law. I had extended family responsibilities but no structural supports to carry them out. Although I was 10,000 miles away from India, my responsibilities to my husband's family did not cease. My husband, as the oldest son in the family, had responsibilities that I had to shoulder. I had to take care of my husband's family members who lived with me in our household. This problem is not unique to me. It is a particular example of a more general problem that many immigrants experience. Even when Asian immigrant women take up roles and responsibilities demanded of them in this society, they often are required to operate within the framework of traditional cultural norms and maintain the cultural environment of their homeland in the United States. This can create difficulties for the individuals as well as the group. Migration is often marked by intergenerational and gender tensions in families.[32] Cambodian women raising children in the United States are facing cultural conflict when they want to follow traditional cultural scripts learned in Cambodia. Girls in particular are subject to controls that boys are exempt from. News stories have reported of how girls behave one way at school when they are in the company of peers. However, once they come back home they are expected to be a "true daughter" taking care of younger siblings, doing household chores, and obeying the elders in the family. Girls are not encouraged in Cambodia to be independent and free thinkers.[33] Girls growing up in the United States have to walk a family "tightrope." The culture, society, and economy in the United States make it difficult for them to abide by the scripts that their parents had to follow when in Cambodia. Many mothers I spoke to complained of the excessive freedom children have in this society. As parents they cannot completely insulate their children from the forces of this society nor can they absolutely monitor their children's behavior, especially when they have to work to earn a living to meet the needs of their families. This situation creates ambivalence in them wherein on the one hand they experience and enjoy freedom themselves while at the same time they want to perpetuate Khmer gender traditions and norms of behavior in their children, especially their daughters. The issues they face will be examined more fully later.

The Aim of This Study

Migration to a new country, whether voluntary or involuntary, poses challenges and problems of adaptation. Migration also necessitates adaptation. As migrants have relocated in the communities they have been settled into, they have had to interact with the larger host society. They have been confronted with unanticipated issues, of making choices of what to retain of their traditions and culture as they adapt to the new situations and what to reject and give up. No culture is static. Change is ubiquitous and constant, and the people who have migrated to the United States soon realize that the life they lived in their home country is different from the life here. Some things are difficult to retain and replicate despite the intense desire to keep traditions. Others things are a matter of preference and choice. People adapt to the environment they are placed in and also shape it with their actions and choices. Thus, newcomers to this land adopt many existing customs and institutions. But they also introduce some of their own ethnic practices, thus contributing to the increasing enrichment of the American society and culture. Examples of this will be provided later.

    Cambodian women who came as refugees to the United States and settled in Lowell, Massachusetts are the focus of this study. Approximately 150,000 Cambodian refugees have been admitted to the United States for resettlement since 1979.[34] The largest numbers of these settled in Long Beach, California, and the next largest concentration is in the city of Lowell, Massachusetts. Fifty percent of the total number of Cambodians residing in Massachusetts, according to the 2000 U.S. Census are concentrated in Lowell. Although the official census figures seem to be an undercount, when compared to the newspaper accounts, the fact remains that Cambodians domiciled in Lowell comprise the largest number of Southeast Asians in Massachusetts.

The main focus of this study is to explore and examine the experiences and problems faced by Cambodian women as they have attempted to settle and carve a niche for themselves in the United States, their adopted homeland. There are two reasons for this. First, large numbers of Cambodians who came into this country were women with dependent children. This was the legacy of war that made them refugees in the first place. Following the war experience, the sex ratio of the U.S. Cambodian community is such that women significantly outnumber men as heads of households. Furthermore, the problem of "fitting in" is much greater for women as they try to cope with their traditional gender roles and also mesh with the demands made of them in a new and different society with its distinctively different cultural milieu.

As people migrate from one region to another, they bring with them their cultural heritage. It is part of their identity and existence. Yet they are expected, as reported by one author, to leave their "cultural baggage" as if it is indeed a baggage to be left or carried on at will. The truth is just the opposite. The history of immigration indicates that first generation immigrants have attempted to hold onto their cultural traditions in the face of pressures to assimilate into American values and behavior. This was true of the first wave of European immigrants who came to settle here, and it is still true of newcomers who have come more recently. Indeed, for some new immigrants, the issue of preserving culture is identical to the issue of survival. This is reflected in the response of a Cambodian refugee in his mid fifties who reported "I want to preserve the culture . . . that's the most important thing: to keep the culture alive." When newcomers such as the Cambodians are brought into contact with mainstream Americans, they are faced with U.S. norms and institutions that are very different from what they were accustomed to. This poses a challenge for them as well as the host society that they are settling down to. Aside from demands on resources that the city has to provide for its new residents, there are other cultural and social issues that have to be addressed alongside in accepting the new culturally distinct residents. A case in point is the whole issue of bilingual education that emerged with the large influx of Cambodian refugees into Lowell. This was a polarizing point for many Americans who were for "English only" in America. Many Americans fail to understand why Cambodians (and other immigrants) do not act as Americans when in the United States. This is not such a simple issue; it is complex. It involves the question of maintaining one's ethnic identity and thereby ensuring one's cultural survival. It also involves the lack of a knowledge base of appropriate skills and information. Indeed, this has to be recognized if such a group having lived through the war trauma of cultural genocide and physical annihilation is to be aided in the process of adaptation and participation in U.S. culture and society.

As an immigrant educated in English schools in India, speaking the language fluently, and having a knowledge and exposure to Western culture and values, I remember the problem in graduate school of understanding the professors initially who spoke English "the American way." How much more difficult and problematic it must be for a people who have no knowledge of English and are thrust into U.S. society? For them, coming to America is like traveling in time, arriving at a historical period without being prepared for it. Not only have these people traveled many miles away from their native country, they have also traveled centuries in one big leap. Their "cultural knowledge," which is substantially different from the mainstream norms and values that characterize U.S. society, is likely to make the process of adaptation somewhat problematic for them. For example, obedience to elders such as parents and teachers, conformity to the traditional familial values and behavior, lack of assertiveness and aggression even in the face of opposition, and abiding by teachings of Buddha are fundamental to the Cambodian (Khmer) people. Pursuit of individuality and personal freedom, display of assertiveness and aggression in social interaction, and dating as a prelude to marriage are alien to their culture. It can be assumed that these disparate cultural values, when juxtaposed together, are likely to create both internal and external difficulties, for those whose early socialization provided them with blueprints for behavior other than what is expected in the new country.

What does it mean to be Cambodian and what are the problems inherent in attempting to retain cultural practices that define them as such? What factors facilitate and/or impede adaptation as they attempt to retain their ethnic identity while at the same time also be a part of U.S. society? What issues emerge as the second generation grows up and is sandwiched between the contradictory demands and expectations of their parents and peers and the world that surrounds them? These are questions of interest in this study. Understanding these problems, processes and patterns of adaptation and adjustments of Cambodian women in their new habitat in Lowell is the focus of this research. As I have come in contact with Cambodian women who have come as refugees to this country, I have been amazed by the resilience of those who, despite events surrounding their lives, have demonstrated the determination and the will to succeed. At the same time, there are those for whom life has been an endless struggle: The problems they face are immense, and resources to cope with them are minimal. They experience the pressures to change, to fit in and to abandon the traditional ways of behaving if they are to "make it" in America. At the same time, those who change in order to fit in also experience the pressure to conform to Khmer traditions and not doing so is meted with negativity. For example, "being Americanized" carries with it a negative label as in the case of a Cambodian woman who reported that she was seen to be so Americanized as if "she was born here . . . the way she talks . . . the way she eats, the way she acts." Coming to America has presented a mixed blessing. For many it has been a liberating experience. Those who have "made it" concede they now have the opportunity to weave a new life and existence of happiness, hope, and peace. "It is a chance for a new life," as one refugee is quoted. But to be able to make a new beginning demands that they learn new skills, new rules and roles and values commensurate with their new situation. And herein lies the challenge for these new migrants.

Why I Chose Cambodians

My interest in studying Cambodians evolved out of an array of circumstances—personal, professional, and accidental. As an immigrant I have personal interest in the subject of immigration and immigrants. But my interest also has professional origins. I have been fortunate to teach in Lowell, a city that earned the title of an All America City because of its cultural distinctiveness and social history. Lowell is situated north of Boston, Massachusetts, and can serve as a prototype for U.S. ethnic history. Since its inception as an urban center in the second decade of the nineteenth century, it has attracted people from various places, domestic and foreign, who came to it in search of work, settled here, adopted its institutions and culture while also shaping it. The ethnic history of Lowell is indeed the story of "Immigrant America." There lies its uniqueness. As one peruses through its social history, one becomes aware of the variety of ethnic groups that found shelter in Lowell and the forces and the processes that aided them in retaining their ethnic identity while adapting to American society and culture.

The opportunity to first understand the importance of Lowell in the development of U.S. society came several years ago when I participated in a grant funded by the National Endowment of Humanities. This was a grant where the focus of study was the city of Lowell, its birth, growth, and development, from an interdisciplinary point of view from the time it was first founded in the 1820s to the third quarter of the twentieth century, the time of the grant. Participation in the grant enhanced my understanding of the role of the economic forces in the growth and development of Lowell as an industrial center. It also provided me the opportunity to learn about the ethnic history of Lowell and the role different ethnic groups played in shaping Lowell as an urbanindustrial center. The study of the social history of Lowell led me to discover the gold mine it was for studying ethnicity and ethnic groups. Lowell is a natural laboratory for studying "Immigrant America." This was further reinforced and sharpened when I was invited to develop and team teach an interdisciplinary honors course on Ethnicity in Massachusetts where faculty from different disciplines from different campuses in the University of Massachusetts system shared their expertise and knowledge of ethnic groups of interest to them. The rich historical resources of the National Historical Park at Lowell were used as teaching and learning tools by both the faculty and students involved with this course. The examination of different ethnic groups at different historical times settled in Lowell underscored the problems and processes of assimilation encountered by them in sharp focus.

The most recent people to settle in Lowell have come from Southeast Asia, the bulk of whom are refugees from the war-ravaged country of Cambodia. My interest in studying them was first spurred by a Cambodian student who wanted me to write about the refugee experiences and the journeys made by refugees en route to the United States. It was first through her that I learned firsthand the trauma and the difficulties she and many of her compatriots had experienced with the war taking place in that region. It was the war and the subsequent political turmoil that resulted from it that led her first to the refugee camps and subsequently to Lowell. Around the time I met her, I also heard rumblings in my class from white American students against the new settlers coming into Lowell. Having students of different ethnicities in my class who were so passionately divided on the issue of immigration and the public assistance given to Southeast Asian newcomers to Lowell was the spark that got me interested in learning more about this group. My own ethnic background has also helped me in my choice as I can relate to and understand with ease some of the similarities and differences in journeys made and the dramas enacted as they were played out.

The Research Process and Data Collection

The research for this study started in the mid 1990s, several years after Cambodians started coming to Lowell as refugees. I first encountered people from Cambodia as students in the courses that I was teaching both through the program of Continuing Education and the day school. I began to have glimpses of their experiences as some of them shared their experiences with me or responded to ideas presented in courses I taught. One of them in particular (mentioned earlier) wanted me to write about the Cambodians' experience apprising the world of the horrors they had gone through before they left their homeland. As the numbers of Southeast Asian refugees became visible in Lowell, they also became the objects of envy and suspicion. In one of my classes, many American students of European descent, born and raised here but whose grandparents were immigrants, were very vocal about their opposition to the support that "these people were receiving from the government" while they had to work hard and pay for everything themselves. As a first-generation immigrant of Asian descent, I became interested in learning more about this group of new residents in Lowell and compare them to experiences and information about other communities that I was familiar with. One of the things that surprised me was the apparent speed with which many of these newcomers were beginning to adopt some "American practices" and make their presence felt in the city at large. Politically, they were making their mark. The first Cambodian city councilor in Lowell, Rithy Uong, was elected in 1999. He won a seat at large, which is difficult for immigrant newcomers.[35] In 2001 two Cambodians were contestants in the city elections, one for the School Committee and the other for the City Council. Uong retained his seat in the City Council. Noon, the candidate for the school committee, did not get elected. Others have also campaigned for election to the City Council since then. I have seen flyers posted (in 2005) in the Angkor shopping plaza where many Cambodians shop.

I decided to focus on the experiences of Cambodian women, because "women are the guardians and symbols of tradition in virtually every culture."[36] As stated earlier, there is research evidence that indicates that even when women are assuming new roles, earning incomes that augment familial income, they are still expected to adhere to traditional gender scripts.[37] Personally, I have seen it among many Asian immigrant women as well as the dilemma and stress these exert on the individuals attempting to traverse between two worlds. I have interviewed Cambodian women of different age groups and different classes to ascertain the issues they confront and the ways they attempt to construct identities that define their ethnicity. The interviews provided access to information that sheds light on conflicts and continuity in their social experiences. All the women, despite their differences in social background and age, were refugees and had spent some time in the refugee camps before entering the United States. To that extent, all of them had a shared experience that connected them.

I interviewed twenty-five women between the ages of 16 to 73 who came to Lowell either alone or with families. I reached these women through neworks where one interview snowballed into other interviews. I talked to women, some directly and others through an interpreter, so that I could gain insights into their experiences that would allow me to write about them. I recognize that my inability to speak their language is a limitation. As I interviewed the women, I learned of their personal histories of why and how they came, the difficult journeys they made and what awaited them after coming to the United States. I asked them their views of what it is they like about being here and what it is they do not feel happy about in this country. I have paid special attention to family and gender issues, knowing how hard the first generation tries to replicate the cultural values and institutions of the home country. I have attempted to portray the women essentially as they see themselves and their prospects and problems in this society. I have changed the names of the people I have interviewed in order to conceal their identities but have attempted to truthfully present the information as it was given to me, without changing its content. In writing about the cases and presenting the information in quotes I have tried to present the emotional nuances of the conversation between them and me. Although the sample of women who agreed to participate in this study is small and limited, each one of them nevertheless presents a case, a product of historical time and space that has affected their thinking and actions. The fact that there is a pattern in their responses leads me to believe that these individuals are indeed representing the social and historical forces that have shaped their experiences. Their personal stories are like dots in a cultural maze that, when connected, present a picture—their cultural and social history—that provides the backdrop to understand their personal stories and experiences. In addition to the women who are the main subject of this study, I have also interviewed some community leaders, Cambodian counselors and others who had worked with the community, who are privy to some of the issues confronting the community. The women who provided glimpses of their personal lives were located mainly through students and some parents who are respected in the community for their social standing. Some of the women interviewed were at school working for a degree, and they highlighted some of the issues that pursuing an education entails, especially when parents do not share the same belief system as their children. But these very people also illustrate the factors that allow or provide the opportunity to new residents of the country to "make it in America." Writing about some of these problematic issues in a community is always challenging lest it be misconstrued. I had frequently heard of incidents of premarital pregnancy among Cambodian teenagers from parents who were concerned about their own daughters.[38] But when I sought help from an individual in locating persons in such situations that she knew of, her reaction was "why study them?" Her reasoning for such a question was that this phenomenon is not unique to Cambodians alone. There was a sense of embarrassment and defensiveness in her reaction. It is true that problems Cambodian teens are facing are a part of a larger U.S. problem. There are structural forces in society that affect individuals. My focus is to understand *both* the structural and the cultural factors that facilitate or hinder this group of newcomers to adapt to U.S. society so that both specific and general conclusions can be drawn from their examples.

Growing up to be American is not an easy thing for children of refugees or immigrants where they encounter pressure to assimilate to mainstream society while at the same time also conform to ethnic norms demanded by parents. They too are a "sandwiched generation." The fact that these children and their parents are also burdened with the experience of flight from wartorn home countries only aggravates their problems. According to one report, two out of three Cambodian refugees in the United States have experienced the violent death of a close family member, the highest percentage of any refugee group.[39] It must not be easy for people to embark upon "social journeys" under such circumstances. The women in this study would not have come to this country had it not been for the war raging in their homelands. How they are navigating their lives is of interest to us. The information presented in the pages of this book is the drama of real life as it is lived and experienced by these women in their new habitat. Learning about and understanding this is both challenging and fascinating at the same time. Hopefully, it will also have practical benefits.

CHAPTER TWO

Origins of the Journey: Where They Came from and Why?

Much has been written about the aftermath of U.S. involvement in the Vietnam War in the 20th century. The plight of the Vietnamese refugees attempting escape by boat received national attention some years ago, and there is extensive literature on resettlement of Vietnamese refugees. Yet the inhuman and unimaginable suffering of neighboring Cambodia and the Cambodians also beleaguered by that Southeast Asian war and its ruthless political leadership has begun to receive attention only recently.[1] Several books have been published recently by survivors depicting the horrors and atrocities they witnessed when they were interned in the labor camps of the Khmer Rouge, the communist party that came to power after taking over Cambodia. These people are the survivors of the genocide who lived to apprise the world of their grim experiences. But they also had the misfortune of seeing the torture and killing of their family members and relatives.[2] Having a loved and dear one brutalized and tortured in one's presence in and of itself is traumatic. One woman I interviewed for my study could not continue with the conversation about her father, who had been killed by the Khmer Rouge, because it was so painful and difficult for her. Everyone in my study has known of someone who had been killed by the soldiers of the Pol Pot regime or who had died in the labor camps. To avoid similar fate, these survivors risked their lives in undertaking the hazardous trip through rough and dangerous terrain to escape from Cambodia into neighboring countries that would admit them as refugees. They chose to make the difficult journey into the unknown rather than live in the familiar world of the known that had given them so much pain and suffering. This journey involved walking through the dense jungles and inhospitable territories for hours at a stretch, sometimes crossing rivers at night, in order to avoid detection by the enemy. They walked endlessly with little or no food so that they could find freedom from terror.

The women in this study are among those who successfully undertook the journey that led them to their destination in a refugee camp. They were eventually able to migrate to yet another country, this time the U.S. The description of their escape gives one an understanding of the conditions—the physical hardships and political turmoil—that prompted them to take this tremendous risk. Their stories of escape are described below. But first a brief historical review of the events leading to the situation prompting masses of people to abandon their country for another unknown territory is presented. This provides the context for the journey undertaken by the women in this study, despite heavy odds.

Cambodia and Its People

Cambodia is a small country situated in Southeast Asia bordering the Gulf of Thailand and sharing borders with Thailand (in the northwest), Laos (in the North), and Vietnam (in the southeast). This is shown in Map 1. The country of Cambodia is hedged with rugged mountains and jungles and is comparable in size to the state of Missouri.[3] Its land area is a total of 2,570 kilometers (1,596

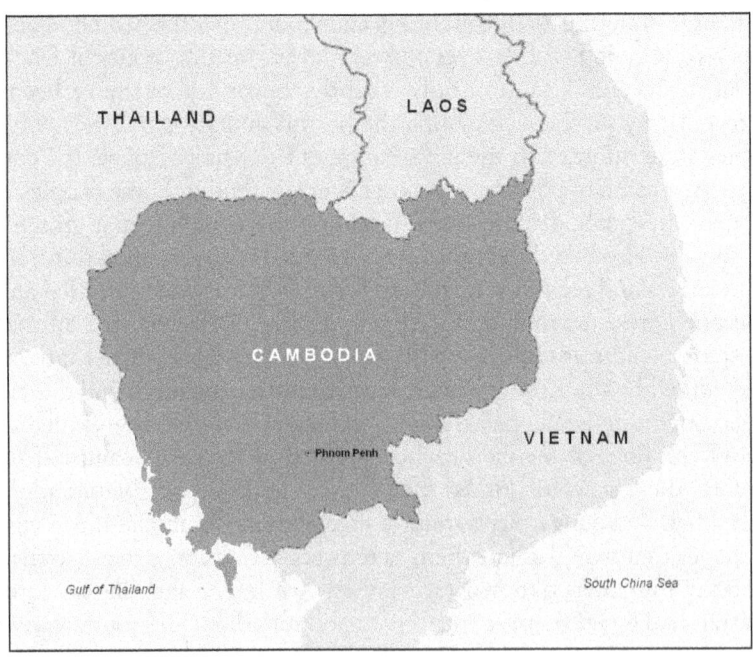

Map 1. Map of Cambodia with Surrounding Southeast Asian Countries

miles). Its population is a little over thirteen and a half million,[4] and its capital is Phnom Penh. Cambodia has a tropical climate and is hot most of the year. The rainy season lasts from May to November, and the dry season is from December to April. It has a rich variety of natural resources, including minerals. A large part of its territory is covered with forest and woodland and 85 percent of its population live in villages, in huts sitting on stilts to protect against the monsoon rains. Cambodia is principally a rural society with the majority of its people engaged in subsistence farming. Before the war, most of the peasants owned some land to meet their subsistence requirements. The family household is the basic social and economic unit of village life. It is the basis of both domestic and economic activities not unlike other societies in history before the advent of industrial capitalism.

The average land ownership per household in Cambodia is four acres nationwide. In general, rural households are self-sufficient. However, household members also participate in exchange of commodities that is part of the national and international trade network.[5] In the early 1960s less than 10 percent of the total peasant population was landless. Due to the collective trauma that the country experienced with the events following the 1975 Khmer Rouge takeover, Cambodia's economy was dramatically affected. It is now slowly recovering, although it is faced with daunting challenges. It is estimated that as much as 40 percent of the population is poor, and 50 percent of its population is less that 20 years of age.[6]

The Cambodian people are known as Khmer. Their official language also is known as Khmer. French and English are also spoken. The majority of its population (90 percent) is ethnically Khmer. The rest consist of Chinese, Vietnamese, and Muslims. Most people in Cambodia are Buddhists subscribing to what is known as Theravada Buddhism. This school of Buddhism claims to perpetuate the true teachings and practices of Buddha and traces its descent from the original *sangha* or community of monks that first followed the Buddha. Theravada Buddhism in Cambodia is interwoven with folk religious beliefs, magical rituals and practices.[7] There are also traces of Hindu gods and goddesses in Cambodian culture because of the influence of Hindu beliefs and practices in Cambodian society with the exchange of trade and commerce occurring between Cambodia and India in the past. Many gods revered in ancient Cambodia are recognizable Indian divinities.[8] However, Hindu beliefs and practices are now thoroughly integrated and interwoven with native Khmer beliefs that for most lay Khmer people they are indistinguishable from Buddhist traditions. The impact of Hindu culture is also discernible in the first names Khmer people have, although phonetic changes have taken place. Many Khmer women that I interviewed had names that are quite common in India. When I asked them of the origin and meaning of their names, only a few were aware of the Indian origin or knew the original meanings of their names.

A Brief History of Cambodia and Cambodian Refugees

Cambodia, or Kampuchea, was relatively unknown to the world at large until it was drawn into the Vietnam War in the 1960s. Historically, it had a glorious past, the results of which are seen in the magnificent ruins of the famous temple—Angkor Wat—in northwestern Cambodia known as Angkor. The Cambodian era of greatness, splendor, and glory started in the ninth century with the founding of the Angkor Empire and lasted through the thirteenth century. During this time Cambodia was ruled by a succession of kings known as *devarajas* or god kings who were seen as the earthly manifestations of Divinity. It is they who unified and expanded the Khmer Empire.[9] The Empire's influence extended over much of Siam (Thailand), Vietnam, and Laos. At the zenith of its glory, the Cambodian Empire was marked by stupendous achievements in culture, architecture, and warfare. However, in the thirteenth century the glory of the Khmer Empire began to decline when two neighboring countries, Thailand and Vietnam, became increasingly powerful and began to fight for control over Cambodia's territory and its population. Persistent invasion of Angkor by its neighbors combined with some other forces contributed to its downfall.[10] From the fourteenth century onward, the Khmer Kingdom was greatly weakened by the expansionist annexation of parts of Cambodian territory by Siam (Thailand) and Vietnam. Cambodia was wedged between these two internecine countries and alternately attempted to placate both in an effort to maintain its diminishing sovereignty. Its strength was further undermined by internal rivalry and feuds among the members of the royal family vying for the throne. This drama continued for some time until new participants entered the scene that further eroded its autonomy. In the nineteenth century, Cambodia sought the protection of France in an effort to protect its interest from its contending neighbors and in so doing ushered in the reign of a foreign power in Cambodian society. France, already a power broker in the region, was deeply involved in Vietnam during that time.

The political control of Cambodia shifted to France in the second half of the nineteenth century. Cambodia first became a protectorate of France in 1863, and in 1884 it became its colony. As its protectorate France had agreed to protect Cambodia from any claims made on its territory by its neighbors in exchange for money collected through taxes. But this was a ploy for greater control over Cambodian resources. Conflict ensued. The peasantry revolted against the French and some factions of the royal family led them in the fight. Eventually, then King Norodom, in an effort to keep his throne from falling into the hands of his rivals, allowed the French to rule Cambodia. Cambodia became a colony of France, although the monarchy was retained. But the king now had only ceremonial functions. The real power resided in Paris. This pattern was to repeat itself in the years to come when Cambodian leaders sought outside help to protect their own interests in the name of protecting the country by nullifying the efforts of the people who actually wanted to free it from foreign clutches.[11]

The French colonization of Cambodia did not bring the benefits to the Khmer people that normally accrue to a colonized country when brought in contact with a colonizing power. Instead, life continued without much educational or economic improvement for the large majority of people. The French did not introduce the French language to the masses in Cambodia to create a pool of workers for its bureaucratic machinery like the British introduced English in India to train a class of civil servants who would help them govern the country. Instead, the French brought the Vietnamese into Cambodia to help them rule the Cambodians. The Vietnamese knew the French language and the French system of governance. In 1943 more than half the population of Phnom Penh, the capital of Cambodia, was ethnically Vietnamese in origin.[12] Similarly, the revenue Cambodia was generating in the mid-1930s through its rice exports and rubber plantations was not filtering down to its masses. The benefits of the economic boom in these industries accrued to the French and the Chinese, who monopolized the export trade under the French rule in Cambodia. The majority of Cambodian people remained agrarian, untouched by modern forces that colonialism brought. This may have given rise to the sense of timelessness that Cambodia has been credited with. Yet some scholars of Cambodian history have suggested that it is misleading to portray Cambodian society as changeless.[13] Indeed, behind the façade of tranquillity significant changes were in the offing. These provide the backdrop for the events in the last quarter of the twentieth century that catapulted the country into political turmoil and tragedy.

The Second World War marked a watershed in the history of Cambodia vis-à-vis its relation to the French. The war had greatly weakened France. Japanese involvement in the war in that region against the French strengthened Cambodian demand for independence. For the first time Cambodians began to express ideas publicly. Political activity and parties sprang up. Buddhist clergy who were opposed to French rule played a crucial role in the burgeoning movement against colonial hegemony. The French on their part crowned Prince Sihanouk as the king in lieu of its rightful heir because they thought he was malleable. At the time of his accession to the throne he was nineteen years old. However, he turned out to be much more politically astute than he was envisioned to be and outwitted the French by his political cunning. Like his grandfather earlier, he was willing to let the French rule Cambodia as long as he remained king. However, as the demand for national independence gained momentum after the Second World War, there were several individuals who became serious contenders to political leadership in Cambodia who were also opposed to the institution of monarchy. Sihanouk outmaneuvered them in a series of clever political moves by first removing his opponents and then bluffing the French into caving into his demand for freedom. In so doing, he was able to wrest control of Cambodia from France while at the same time keeping his throne intact. He was amply aided by the growth of nationalistic consciousness among the young students who had been exposed to the democratic ideas of the French Revolution and their growing disaffection with the foreigners (French, Vietnamese, and Chinese) who dominated the Cambodian economy.

Cambodia gained its independence from the French in 1953. But this did not end its political woes or interference from foreign governments. Sihanouk dominated Cambodia for the next fifteen years. He attempted to keep Cambodia free of any conflict that was raging in Indochina and was successful in keeping Cambodia neutral by pitting the United States, Soviet Russia, and China against one another. However, his politics and policies were not geared toward the welfare and advancement of the country; rather, their purpose was to ensure his political monopoly. He did not allow democratic rule and political participation of the people in the country. Any dissent and political opposition was likened to being anti-Cambodian.[14] Sihanouk claimed "Cambodia was a democracy," but he "ruled it like a medieval monarch."[15] His vision of Cambodia was that of a traditional rural society woven around Buddhist norms and values, and he attempted to steer the country toward his desired goal. To achieve this end, he allocated a large percentage of funds for education, far more than was normal for a developing country. Many people in the villages did get an education as a result. However, the knowledge they received did not enhance their future in the agricultural sector, but rather gave them the ammunition and know-how to understand and challenge the wisdom of the policies adopted by Sihanouk. Sihanouk's policies had increasingly divided the country along class-ethnic cleavages with coveted positions and rewards going to those who were loyal to him. The chasm between the villages and the cities widened also. As this happened, the divisions between the rich and the poor increased and so did the mutual suspicion among them. Sihanouk's lack of sound economic policies that could have helped modernize Cambodian economy, and his intolerance of political dissent coupled with his romantic although unrealistic dream of retrieving the past glory of Cambodian society created disillusionment in many against his rule. The war in Vietnam, the induction of the young intellectuals into the growing communist party, the corruption in his government, the disenchantment of the elite with his rule, and the financial trouble he led his country into only hastened his political demise. In a 1970 bloodless coup led by his deputy Lon Nol, who had the backing of United States, Sihanouk was ousted from his position as head of the state. At that time he was out of the country. With his removal from office, Cambodia descended into an abysmal calamity.

Soon after Sihanouk's displacement from power there was hope and optimism expressed by the new leadership of putting the Cambodian house in order and restore peace and stability in the country. Instead, Cambodia was enveloped in a state of turmoil and chaos, and conditions became increasingly worse. Lon Nol did not have the political acumen of his deposed predecessor. He had miscalculated his own strength and that of his opponents. After coming to power, he abandoned the policy of neutrality pursued by Sihanouk that had kept Cambodia out of the Indochina war. Lon Nol's effort to get the Vietnamese communists off Cambodian soil led to a series of border clashes with neighboring North Vietnamese forces, who were far better trained and equipped for military operation. Lon Nol's army was ill prepared and unequipped to fight against the Vietnamese communists and lost large portions of Cambodian soil to the North Vietnamese—so much so that more than half the country slipped under the control of North Vietnamese army.[16] The escalating conflict also gave rise to uprooting of people from their homes and villages. Phnom Penh was deluged with refugees seeking shelter from the conflict.

As the conflict and military operations intensified, Lon Nol found himself in a very difficult and precarious situation. With American bombing of communist sanctuaries within Cambodia, the Vietnamese were making deeper incursions into Cambodian territory. While Lon Nol was battling North Vietnamese communist forces, he was confronted with opposition from the Cambodian communists known as the Khmer Rouge under the leadership of Saloth Sar, their emergent leader who later would be known by the world for his horrific acts against humanity. The Khmer Rouge were consolidating their hold in Cambodia under the leadership of Sar. The Communist Party of Kampuchea (CPK), led by Sar, joined hands with Sihaouk's forces to fight against Lon Nol's government. Although Lon Nol had removed Sihanouk from power, he was unable to eliminate Sihanouk completely. Sihanouk had called for resistance to Lon Nol's government. He allied himself with his former archenemies, the most famous of whom was Saloth Sar, later known as Pol Pot. They came together under the banner of National United Front of Cambodia. Sihanouk was the figurehead of this movement for national liberation. But the actual power rested in the hands of the top cadre of the Cambodian Communist Party, who were operating from within the country and increasing their influence in the countryside. They had disdain for Sihanouk but accepted him as a titular head for pragmatic reasons, to win support of the peasants among whom he was popular. In fact, the Khmer Rouge used Sihanouk's popularity to recruit young people into the coalition movement without disclosing their own identity.[17]

The Phnom Penh government of Lon Nol was thus under siege from both internal and external enemies. The spread of the Vietnam War into Cambodia, the bombing of communist sanctuaries in Cambodia by the United States, and the alliance forged between Sihanouk and Saloth Sar to topple the government of Lon Nol threatened the very fabric of Cambodian society. On the one hand, the Cambodian army was engaged in armed conflict with the North Vietnamese. On the other hand, it was losing ground at home to the Cambodian communists who were strengthening their hold in the countryside. The latter were disciplined and focused and were willing to subject their rank and file to extreme hardship to attain the goal they had set out for themselves, namely a revolution to restore Cambodian society to its past glory. The government of Lon Nol, on the other hand, was corrupt, disorganized, and in a state of disarray. His army had grown in size due to the recruitment of many that responded to his call for a holy war to preserve Khmer people and culture. However, it was no match for organized and disciplined forces of the Vietnamese communists or the communists at home. Consequently, Lon Nol's army lost major battles. Corruption and incompetence was rampant. Cambodian society was already in a state of disintegration even before Khmer Rouge came to power.[18]

The Vietnamese forces withdrew from Cambodian territory when the peace accord was reached between United States and Vietnam in 1973. The war in Cambodia now involved two Cambodian armies, those of Lon Nol and Saloth Sar, fighting against each other. The Khmer Rouge, knowing their strength, had refused to negotiate with Lon Nol and emerged as the new ruler on the Cambodian scene. When the Lon Nol forces were engaged in armed conflict with the Vietnamese communists, the Cambodian communists were organizing villages under their control as cooperatives with everything controlled by the party cadre. These cooperatives were organized as part of the war effort. Food production and distribution was no longer left to individuals engaged in the activity. Rather, these were controlled and managed by the party. People living in these villages were under strict surveillance and no movement of those inside these collectives was permitted without prior approval. Any attempt to the contrary was meted with severe punishment. People started "disappearing." This was the model that was followed on the national scale after Saloth Sar came to power in 1975. Only it was far more rigid and ruthless.

1975–1979: The Khmer Rouge Years

After the communist victory over Lon Nol's government, Saloth Sar became the revolutionary leader of Cambodia. It was then that he officially changed his name to Pol Pot.[19] Cambodia's new name became Democratic Kampuchea (DK), but there was nothing democratic about the new regime under Pol Pot. The Khmer revolution in Cambodia did not bring freedom from poverty and inequality as promised by the party cadre when recruitment efforts were under way in the countryside before the fall of Lon Nol's government. On the contrary, the entire country was now treated as a massive pool of slave labor, and people were ordered to put in grueling and long hours of work with very little food or rest in between. Hunger and starvation was endemic. People survived on a daily watery bowl of rice despite the long hours of work they put in the labor camps. Even children were not spared. Life was hard and arduous under the Khmer Rouge regime. There was no free or personal time. In fact, there was no time for anything but work. People were called upon to make sacrifices to build a Cambodia that would be self-sufficient and meet its food and other requirements without outside international aid. People were literally expected to work sometimes with bare hands in the fields, or at construction sites to build roads, dams, or irrigation canals. There are reports of people having to work between fourteen and eighteen hours a day.[20] Work started very early before sunrise and continued till late in the evening. Anyone caught resting or taking a break was punished severely with a more and difficult work assignment. One of my informants who worked in the labor camp reported that even after work ended, sometimes they had to attend meetings called by the Angka (organization) that were like indoctrination sessions. Children and adults alike had to work for the production of public goods. Nothing was private or personal. In order to infuse such a rigorous schedule, fear and suspicion were instilled in the minds of people. No one could be trusted. The rule of terror was instituted, and no disagreement of any kind was permitted. Soldiers patrolled regularly to ensure that their orders were followed. Obedience to the Angka was emphasized. Parents cautioned their children to keep quite lest they say something inadvertently that could give away their former identity and thus imperil the lives of the whole family. Some who had previously worked under Lon Nol's government voluntarily separated from their families to ensure their safety, knowing that if they were discovered to be related all would be killed. One man is quoted to have said, "If I stay with you, a lot of people know me and they will kill all of us."[21] Even so, tales of horror and terror became commonplace. Some people were inhumanly tortured to force a confession that would eventually lead to their execution, even though they were not guilty of the "crime" they were suspected of.

At the time the Khmer Rouge army marched into Phnom Penh after its government fell, the residents of the city who were weary of the war were glad that it was over and enthusiastically greeted them with applause. However, they were unaware of the fate that awaited them. Immediately after taking over Phnom Penh, the grim-faced the Khmer Rouge soldiers brandishing revolvers and AK-47s, in black dreary attire, ordered all citizens to leave their homes. They announced on large horns "Take as little as you can! You will be able to return in three days."[22] On the first day of victory, a massive and forced evacuation of people to the countryside was ordered from all the urban centers of Cambodia. People were removed from their homes, men and women, young and old, and were taken to distant places to start a new life under the disciplinary norms of the new revolutionary government. Under the new "Democratic" Kampuchea, all class distinctions would be eliminated and Cambodia would be turned into one "large work camp." People had to leave almost all their worldly possessions except a few valuables that could be hidden in the helm or secret pocket of the sarong. Some even hid their valuables and jewelry for safekeeping while they were gone. Families hastily packed their clothing, medicine, and food for the journey, not knowing where and for how long they would be away. They took what little food or clothing they could carry with them. There was no time for much else as no advance notice for preparation was given. As people were forced out of their homes or offices, they were made to go in the direction they had exited the building. A woman I interviewed was a nurse in Cambodia and worked as a midwife in a hospital in Phnom Penh. She stated that she and others who were in the hospital on that fateful day were forced to move out of the hospital following a road in the direction of a camp closest to the point of exit they had come out of. She and others who worked there were not even allowed to go home to contact their family members. Most people were walking; some were driving in motor vehicles or carts away from their homes or workplaces toward the outskirts of the city and beyond. Even the sick and the invalid were not spared. The sick from the city hospitals were among the first to be pulled out into the streets to march to unknown and uncertain futures.[23] Columns of people jammed the streets, as they were forced to migrate to destinations in the countryside. People were moved from cities, towns, and villages as well in order to control the total population and thwart any attempt at rebellion. As the evacuation proceeded, people were herded like goats and sheep and sent to live in "cooperatives." Many young and old never made it, succumbing to fatigue, fever, and hunger and dying by the wayside. Many others were killed for behavior seen as recalcitrant by the soldiers. Hours after the revolutionary takeover Phnom Penh was empty and quite bereft of people.

Upon arrival at the village camp, people had to undergo screening to ascertain their past histories. They were assigned huts for living, given new drab clothes to wear to emphasize uniformity and equality among the people, and given eating bowls and spoons. They were also given instructions about appropriate behavior and what was expected of them. Those who were seen to be associates of the "enemy" were sent away and never seen again. These included professionals, intellectuals and former government officials, and military personnel. People were even sent away for such absurd reasons as wearing glasses, taken to be a sign of being educated. Those who were not killed were used as slave labor for the construction of a new modern Cambodia. Older children were separated from their parents. Families lived in huts and had to eat in communal kitchens where they were served scanty meals at specified times. If one was late for a meal, there was nothing available to eat until the next meal. The food was rationed, and people were given very little to eat. Hunger and starvation were rampant. So was death. All the women I interviewed for this study spoke of how hungry they were all the time because of how little they were given to eat in the labor camps, although they had to work long hard hours from dawn until late in the evening. Some of these women were children at the time when they were forcibly sent into the labor camps.

The two important institutions that were essential building blocks of Cambodian society were attacked and targeted for destruction by the DK regime. These were the family/household and religion. "From 1975 to 1979 the Khmer Rouge regime not only upended the entire Buddhist religion but also mounted history's fiercest ever attack on family life."[24] In separating family members and banning any romance and loyalty among them, the party cadre aimed at destroying the family as a way to achieve their revolutionary goals. Young people were separated from adult family members in an effort to replace family bonds with loyalty to the revolutionary state. Children were taught to use value neutral terms of kin address instead of traditional kin terms used to address parents and elders. Use of such terms as *mae* (mother) and *ov* (father) were to be preceded by *mit* (friend) to subvert family loyalty.[25] Children were even encouraged to spy and tell upon their parents.

Just as the family was targeted for attack to achieve revolutionary goal of Pol Pot's regime, so was the Buddhist religion viewed as an anathema for the revolution and thus targeted for weeding out. The Buddhist value system, an integral part of Cambodian way of life, had to be destroyed if the revolution was to be successful. Early on the DK regime attempted to replace Buddhist values with the political ideology of the revolution. Buddhist monks were seen as parasites living off the labor of others. Buddhist monks, who refused to leave the order, were killed after severe torture and many were taken to work as slave labor in the work camps of the Khmer Rouge to build a new "democratic" Cambodia. Temples were destroyed and desecrated, and what is worse, many temple sites became the venues for execution and torture.[26]

Untold miseries and unimaginable hardships were borne by citizens of Cambodia during the years of DK regime, which lasted from 1975 to 1979. Those who survived the ghoulish nightmare had gory tales to tell of their experiences in these horror camps. Their stories were essentially similar. Others less fortunate met a cruel or a violent death. Individuals were isolated from one another such that no friendship or solidarity could develop among them. Secrecy was the norm and anyone asking or questioning was seen as a potential or actual enemy. Those suspected of harboring protest were killed brutally, sometimes in the presence of or within the hearing distance of their loved ones. Gruesome stories are documented where, after being killed, organs from the bodies of victims were pulled out to show family members what a "bad" example looked like.[27] Some two million people, a fourth of Cambodia's population, died during this time. Death was either due to torture and execution or hunger, starvation, and sickness. Some, unable to bear the hardship required of them, committed suicide. Others sought escape into neighboring countries as a way to end this terrible life. Many attempted to cross into Thailand to seek shelter in the refugee camps there. Of course, this journey was fraught with danger and discovery would have imperiled the lives of those who embarked upon this dangerous course. Many, of course, did attempt to escape. The journey undertaken by the women in this study who made it to safety is described in the next section.

The Great Escape

The political revolution under the aegis of Khmer Rouge described above, with its torture and execution within the "killing fields" of Cambodia, eventually led to a mass exodus of people to countries sharing its borders. From there these refugees were rerouted to countries in the western hemisphere that agreed to take them. Many were admitted to the United States. The journeys the Cambodian refugees made as they escaped from Cambodia to the refugee camps and then finally to their destination in the United States are cited here.

People who made it to safety shared some common experiences. Like the experiences of the people in the labor camps, the stories of escape are also strikingly similar. When the women in this study described their journeys from the labor camps to the refugee camps, en route to the United States, their host country that accepted them, this became strikingly evident. Their ordeal began in April 1975 after Khmer Rouge forces came to power and lasted through 1979 when the Vietnamese army defeated the Khmer Rouge forces and liberated Cambodia from the clutches of Pol Pot's evil and cruel regime. As these people were forcibly evacuated from their homes in the cities or towns they lived in, they had to withstand severe hardships due to conditions imposed upon them (cited in the preceding section). Many of them were children at that time ranging between the ages of three to thirteen. Their stories are cited below.

Reasmei was only three years old when her family was forced out of its home in Phnom Penh. Her father was a high school teacher. They had a comfortable life before the revolution and came from a middle-class background. Reasmei is ethnically Sino-Khmer with a light skin. Her father is Chinese and her mother Khmer. Unlike her, her mother has brown skin. It has been noted that in Cambodia intermarriage between the Chinese and the Khmer was not uncommon, and many of these people with dual ethnic heritage identified themselves as either Khmer or Chinese. Reasmei identifies herself as Khmer and spoke that language at home with her parents.

After the fall of Phnom Penh, her family was evacuated from their home. They had to travel by road and train from Phnom Penh to Battambong where they were finally relocated in a concentration camp. Life was very hard in the camp, and there was not enough food to eat. Her mother stitched clothes for the village camp and also worked in the rice fields. Her father cooked in the concentration camp. It was his cooking skills that saved his life. It is possible that he concealed his educational background to escape the fate meted out to those with education. It was not unusual for people to do so. A Cambodian man, a school teacher in the Lowell school system, recalled that he lied about his education when asked about his background. It was this lie that saved his life.[28] Loung Ung, in her memoirs, writes about the deliberate efforts that her parents made to conceal their roots and upbringing in order to save their lives. She was only five years old when she was evacuated from her home and moved into the labor camps, but was aware of the danger of disclosing her father's background.[29] She and her siblings were instructed by her parents not to talk lest they give away their identity and thus endanger their lives. Even her mother did minimal talking to conceal her Chinese accent.

Reasmei spent four years in the concentration camp with her parents. After the Vietnamese liberated Cambodia, she returned to Phnom Penh with her family to find their house an empty building. In 1979 they left Cambodia. They walked, rode in an ox cart, traveled by boat, and hired guides to help them in their journey out of Cambodia. On the way sometimes they took shelter with families they knew. They traveled day and night and after a month arrived in a refugee camp in Thailand. The camp was very crowded. They were given food, cooking utensils, and a hut to live in. Getting food was hard. It was in this camp that Reasmei had a life with some semblance of normality. She could play again with children her own age. She also started school, learning math and Khmer in the camp. She along with her family stayed in this camp for a year and a half. While in Thailand they were moved to three different camps, the last one being particularly bad with open spaces, no privacy, and little help given to new arrivals. Sometimes the guards in the refugee camps were abusive toward the inmates of the camp and did not shield them from harm.

In total, Reasmei spent more than two years in refugee camps in Thailand. Her family had initially planned to move to Indonesia, but with her mother's impending childbirth those plans had to be abandoned at that time. Her brother was born in Bangkok where her mother had gone for the delivery. They were running out of their money. Some relatives living abroad helped them with money they sent them in the camp. It was through relatives that her mother came to know a monk who brought them food and money in the camp in Thailand. After the birth of her brother, Reasmei and her family moved to Indonesia and lived there for six months. In Indonesia the houses were better than those available in the refugee camps in Thailand. They also had a small plot in which her mother planted Asian vegetables. While in Indonesia Reasei learned some English, words like "hello" and "good morning" and at times also got to watch some films. It was in Indonesia that preparations for coming to the United States got underway. The family left for Singapore by boat. After spending two nights there, they left for the United States to arrive in Los Angeles. This was her first experience at flying and she was scared and felt sick. From Los Angeles the family flew to Oregon to meet up with her mother's relatives who lived there. From their departure from Cambodia to their arrival in United States they had spend several years in different camps in two different countries, but finally they made it to safety and got a chance for a new beginning in a new land far away from their homeland where life had been painful and difficult with no assured guarantee of physical safety and welfare. She and her family were among the fortunate ones who were able to settle down to a life of normalcy in the United States. When I met Reasmei, she was in her early twenties, studying in college for a bachelor's degree and also working part time. Her mother ran a day care business at home and her father was a government employee. Despite the difficult and dangerous experience that had surrounded them in the labor camps of Cambodia, they have made it to safety and have made a new beginning in their adopted land that they call home now.

Mak came to this country when she was fifteen years old. Her father was a rice farmer and her family lived in a village close to the Thai border. Her father was middle range farmer, owned some farmland, and produced vegetables and rice in different villages. Life was comfortable and they lived in a big wooden house. All this changed when the Khmer Rouge took over the country. The entire population in their village was moved to a different area where they were forced to work in labor camps for twelve to fourteen hours a day. Work began early at five o'clock in the morning. After putting long hours of work for the day, they had to attend meetings after dinner that lasted till midnight. There was not enough rest and not enough food for every one. Starvation was common. Work was hard. Mak was assigned such chores as weeding in the rice fields. If she got wet while working in the field, there was no spare clothing available for changing. Sometimes she developed a rash from working in the fields. She was also assigned the arduous work of digging canals. The authorities did not make any concessions for age as far as work was concerned, and children and adults alike had to work in the labor camps. She was forbidden to talk to her siblings. Families were separated by age and sex and assigned to communal living arrangements. The Khmer Rouge soldiers took her fourteen-year-old sister away. Mak was separated from her parents when she was eight years old. She was assigned to a different camp than her parents. It was after a year that she was reunited with her parents when the Vietnamese invaded Cambodia and she was able to join her parents in their village. There are accounts available of survivors of the Cambodian revolution where parents were separated from their children, siblings from each other and husbands from their wives. Sometimes they never found each other and were presumed to be dead. On other occasions searches for missing family members ended in reuniting the family. In my study several women reported being separated from their family members when the forced evacuation took place in April 1975. The midwife nurse mentioned above happened to bring her daughter to the hospital on that eventful day because her husband, who normally took care of the child in her absence, was held at work. Consequently, at the time of evacuation she had her daughter with her. However, she was separated from her husband on the day that Khmer Rouge forces marched into Phnom Penh and saw him again many years later in the United States. Mak, however, joined her parents after a year's separation from them. Together they attempted leaving Cambodia into neighboring Thailand.

The first time Mak and her family attempted escape from Cambodia they were not successful. The Thai government, fearing the pressure refugees would pose on its resources, turned people away. She, her parents, and two siblings were sent back by bus and dropped near a mountainous region between the border of Thailand and Cambodia. However, her father was able to arrange for two of his children to remain in Thailand. This was his attempt to save at least some of his children. He knew the return journey was fraught with grave danger to life and liberty, and there was no surety that they would return safely. Walking back into Cambodia itself was a blood-curdling and life-threatening experience, Mak recalled. She and many others had to walk down a very narrow path through a mine-infested field where any wrong step could have ended her life. There were corpses lying on the edges of the road, some decomposed and the bodies all swollen. After returning to Cambodia, a second attempt at escape was made and was successfully accomplished. It was her father who decided that the family should seek the safety of the refugee camp rather than remain in Cambodia. He had begun to lose his vision at that time. It was the hardship and fatigue of the labor camp that was taking a toll on the family and may have prompted their decision to leave Cambodia for Thailand. The escape party pretended that they were going fishing in order to avoid detection. She had to hide from soldiers who came after her and walk for two days and night through the jungles and mountainous area in order to avoid the traversed road, where there was greater chance of discovery. She finally reached the camp at Khoidang in Thailand along with her family. In Thailand she spent three years—from 1979 to 1982—in the camp. Her youngest sister was born in the camp. From the refugee camp in Thailand Mak came to Boston. Her stepbrother sponsored her family to come to the United States with the help of a Catholic charity organization. It was in Thailand she first learned about the United States. She envisioned this country "to be like heaven" from what she had heard in the camp. She wanted to come to America—and she did.

Marina comes from a well-to-do family. She lived in Phnom Penh. Her father was a highly placed official in the government before the Khmer Rouge takeover. So were many of her relatives. Her mother a schoolteacher in Phnom Penh had wanted the family to leave Cambodia in 1975 before the revolution, but her father did not expect or suspect that they were in any kind of danger. Her family was educated and affluent. She went to school in Phnom Penh and had learned English and French there. After the Khmer Rouge came to power, her father, along with many of her relatives who held influential positions in the government or the army, was killed. So were six of her siblings. She was sent to the concentration camp along with her mother where she was assigned hard labor, building roads or ditches or "carrying heavy loads up to fifty pounds of rice or water to the mountains." She was twelve years old then. Marina laughingly stated "may be this is why my growth was stunted." (Marina is a short woman with a kind gentle face and a light brown skin.) Of course, there could be some truth in the statement, considering that very little food was given to the resident workers of the camp. Even in sickness she said there was no respite from work. Malnutrition and starvation were common. She spent three long years in Pol Pot's labor camp. Her early adolescent life was lived under the tight rule of the Khmer Rouge. When she and her mother decided to escape, the road to freedom was beset with risk and danger. They had to walk for a week through rough terrain before reaching a refugee camp in Thailand, where she spent a year. Life in a refugee camp in Thailand was not easy either. Robbery and theft were common, and the soldiers on guard in the camp were "bad," she said. Peace was still evading her. She had heard of the United States as a rich country and wanted to come here. From Thailand, her mother had written to an uncle who was a monk living in Maryland, and he sponsored her family to come to the United States. After spending a year in the refugee camp in Thailand she finally came to the United States in 1980. It was in Maryland that she first arrived.

Ratana came from an urban background. She was born in Phnom Penh. Her father was a manager of a hotel. At the time of the Khmer Rouge takeover, she was around eight years old. She was separated from her parents and was sent to work in the fields far away. She had to work long hours. Life was difficult and there was little food to eat in the labor camp. She recalled having to work from five in the morning to five in the evening, with no breakfast and very little to eat at lunch. They were given rice soup to eat. She also had to go to meetings where the internees of the camp were told to work hard. By the time she retired for the day, it was past ten at night. She was always very tired. She is still haunted by the bad memories that she had in the camp under the Khmer Rouge.

It was only after the Vietnamese invasion that Ratana found her parents alive in the village. The situation in Cambodia was bad, politically and economically. To this was an added aggravation of a Vietnamese soldier's being interested in her and wanted to marry her. She was around twelve or thirteen years old at the time. To escape from all this, her mother decided to leave Cambodia. Her mother was the stronger parent, and she decided to undertake the journey that would land them in the refugee camps near the Thai border. However, her flight from Cambodia with her parents was difficult and frightening. They had to walk for ten days, sometimes through the jungles and difficult terrain, to avoid mine-infested paths. On their way, they found skeletons, some in sitting positions. There was death all around. As they made their journey, they were very tired. They had seen some people carrying their elderly parents and others abandoning them on the way. Walking through these territories was particularly hard for her mother, because she was afraid of ghosts. Seeing dead bodies on the road just added to the fear. After the long walk, they finally arrived at a camp from which they were later moved. The camp they ultimately found refuge in was farther from the Thai border. She spent five years in this camp and also went to school there. The refugee camp was far better than the communist camp in which she was forced to work as a child. In the refugee camp at least there was some food, such as rice and canned foods, given to the refugees, she said.

Samy was thirteen years old when she left Cambodia for the refugee camp in Thailand. Her father was multilingual and her mother came from a wealthy family. Her mother was very beautiful. She showed me a family picture of her mother and grandmother, which attested to her physical attractiveness. She had spent four years in the labor camps working in the fields planting rice. Her parents also were assigned farming duties, although they were separated from her. Her whole family, including her parents and siblings, escaped from Cambodia. She described the difficult and arduous journey that involved. Her two brothers were younger to her and although they could both walk, what was demanded of them was not commensurate with their age. Her youngest brother was seven years old and she was thirteen when they headed for the refugee camp in Thailand. They walked for three days and three nights before they reached a camp in Thailand. They walked through the forests with wild animals, crossed rivers on foot at night, and took routes that were believed to be safe from land mines. Her mother had a lot of gold, which was paid to a guide for each member of the escape party. It was the guide who navigated them safely to a refugee camp. The little food they had with them was lost when they crossed the river at night. Samy said that in the refugee camps she saw robbers and shooting. Although her family was not victimized, they nevertheless witnessed violence experienced by others. When they got visas to come to this country, she thought she was "coming to heaven but that was not so."

The cases cited above have much in common despite the differences in social and regional backgrounds. Whether the people were educated urban dwellers or affluent government officials, or farmers in the countryside, their routine life and the world they had known had been uprooted, and they were all subjected to the same harrowing experiences of forced labor camp living. They were coerced into labor in the "reconstruction" of a modern Cambodia. They were separated from their loved ones and had witnessed or experienced the loss of life and liberty. Life in the camps was difficult, cruel, and harsh. The people were treated as less than human; those who survived in the camps were hanging onto life through their resilience and sheer luck. The fortunate ones were able to escape to Thailand (some went to Vietnam) and thence to the United States. But this was just the start of the journey that they had embarked upon. The migration to a new land entailed not only the physical move to a new country but also social and cultural changes and adjustments. It was beset with challenges of its own. Of course, compared to what these people had endured at the hands of their own rulers and countrymen, coming out alive from their own country and refugee camps was itself a blessing and a boon. The society that they were coming into was alien and different, and many of the newcomers had mixed emotions and expectations. Nevertheless, the journey ahead in the land that accepted them held the promise of a new beginning and a new life. The task now before them was taking up the pieces and building anew. This is described in the next chapter.

CHAPTER THREE

All-America City

The city of Lowell, Massachusetts, has earned the title of All-America City. This message is displayed prominently on highway signs as one enters the city of Lowell from interstate highway 495. Cambodian residents played an important role in earning this title as will be shown in Chapter Six. Lowell is indeed an immigrant city. It has provided refuge for innumerable people from around the world ever since it was founded in the second decade of the nineteenth century. That it is immigrant friendly among the cities in the United States has been acknowledged in a survey that was done by a national news organization several years ago. It listed Lowell as among the top six cities in the United States that attracted new immigrants. Federal immigration officials reportedly came to Lowell to learn how the city absorbed the numbers of new immigrants with minimal tensions between diverse ethnic groups residing in the city.[1] The importance of this city for immigrants is recorded in a variety of writings both scholarly and popular. Its significance was documented in an article on Acre—a neighborhood of Lowell—in a special issue of the *Time* magazine published in the fall of 1993 devoted to how immigrants are changing the face of America.

Acre has a very interesting ethnic history. This area was donated to a group of Irish laborers who were brought into Lowell as canal diggers by its mill owners in the early part of the nineteenth century. Since then it has served as a gateway to the United States to many of its new residents, who began their lives in the shantytown of Acre before moving up and out of the slums. In the nineteenth century this was true of the Irish and the French Canadians. In the twentieth century, many minorities, such as the Puerto Ricans and the Cambodians, first found housing in this area. As one drives down the roads in Acre, one is more likely to find people of color living in that area. In the 1980s Cambodians constituted 30 percent of its population. Currently, they constitute its largest ethnic group. Map 2 shows the concentration of Cambodians in Acre and other neighborhoods of Lowell. Lowell is far more multiethnic today than it has ever been since its inception as a burgeoning factory town. Many of its residents are recent migrants to the city. A brief description of the city of Lowell and the factors that prompted these newcomers to come and settle in Lowell as their city of choice are given below.

Lowell: From Birth to Rebirth

The ethnic landscape of Lowell has undergone major transformation in the past three decades. This is in conformity with the transitions taking place in the state of Massachusetts as well as the country in general. Since the beginning of the nineteenth century, the coming of the industrial system to Massachusetts spawned the development of many of its cities and provided new opportunities for employment to its people. The abundance of jobs brought large numbers of people from the farms of New England, Canada, and across the Atlantic seaboard. This is particularly true of the city of Lowell, first

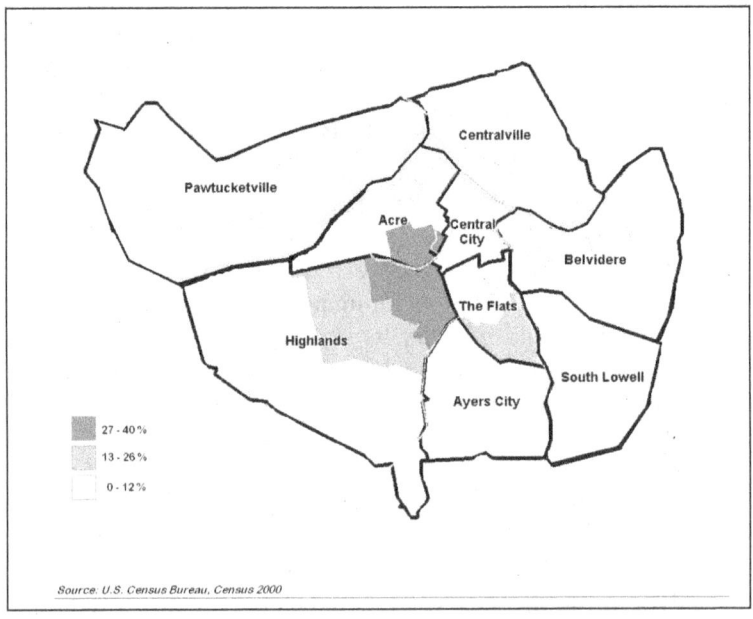

Map 2. Concentration of Cambodians in Neighborhoods of Lowell by Census Tract

planned as a factory town by its corporate owners when it was initially founded as a center for textile manufacturing in the nineteenth century. The coming of the factory system to Lowell provided great opportunities to different ethnic groups who were of European descent. First the Irish, then the French Canadians, and later on Greeks, Poles, and Portuguese appeared in large numbers—so much so that by the end of the nineteenth century as much as 80 percent of the population was foreign born, outnumbering the native-born population in the city. If one peruses through the social history of Lowell, one is likely to find a close connection between its industrial development and its growing immigrant population.

The original workers in the textile mills of Lowell were native-born women from the surrounding New England countryside who were lured into factory work by the attractive wages and living conditions they were provided. But by the middle of the nineteenth century, they began to leave the textile mills in large numbers due to the change in labor policies as they related to working conditions. The first to replace the departing workforce of women were the incoming Irish, followed by the French Canadians, and later other immigrant groups from different parts of Europe. This continued until the first quarter of the twentieth century. By then the city had its distinctive ethnic neighborhoods with the French Canadian, the Greek, the Polish and the Portuguese sections. The population of Lowell, although ethnically diverse, was nevertheless distinctively European in its origin and had registered continuous growth for several decades. In the ninety years between 1830 to 1920 the population of Lowell had grown from a little over 6,000 to almost 113,000. After 1920 its population began to decline with a halt in immigration from Eastern Europe due to the federal laws passed in 1924. With the textile economy faltering and many companies closing down, its population began to decline and continued its downward trend until 1980. In 1980 the population of Lowell was 92,418.[2]

As long as the economy remained stagnant and rates of unemployment were high, there was little incentive for people to come to Lowell. The city's economic fortunes began an upward climb with several developments that ushered in the revitalization of Lowell in the third quarter of the last century. Of particular interest in this process were two interesting and interrelated factors. One had to do with the establishment of the computer industry under the stewardship of An Wang, a Chinese immigrant from Shanghai. Second, the consignment of federal dollars trickling in as areas in Lowell were declared to be part of the National Historical Park contributed to its rejuvenation. This happened in the decade of the 1970s. These developments were crucial for the economic recovery of the city. The regions with high-tech industries were the areas where economic growth was occurring within the state. Lowell was one of such areas. This economic growth coupled with some political initiatives spurred migration into Lowell of new ethnic groups and contributed to its demographic diversity and growth.

Wang, a computer mogul, started the Wang Laboratories, and as the company went public in 1967, its equities soared along with that of its founder. Lowell was the headquarters of the Wang Laboratories, which played a significant role in the city's economic revival. The coming of Wang Industries in Lowell was an asset for its economic growth. Wang had purchased a piece of land in Lowell in 1976, and two years later it became the venue for its corporate headquarters. Wang Industries, a producer of microcomputers and word processing systems, was among the top twenty-six high-tech companies of the state with a net worth of over a million dollars in 1980.[3] Wang Laboratories employed a lot of people with computer skills. In 1982 it was reported to have hired 14,000 local residents. It also was a magnet that drew many other smaller companies that further boosted its economic ascent.[4] The multistory building that housed the company still stands, as a mute testimony to Wang's entrepreneurial ingenuity, although the company is no longer in business.

The urban development of Lowell under the aegis of National Historic Park was crucial for its economic rehabilitation. It brought in federal dollars for cleaning up the city such that it was a safe place for companies doing business there. When I first came to Lowell in the early 1970s, the city was run down with dilapidated buildings. It was an old mill town that had seen better days at one time but was in a state of decline. With the coming of the National Historical Park, the city got a facelift. It was this that brought in people like Wang to come to Lowell.[5] The huge sums of money that was pumped into Lowell beginning in 1978 brought in urban renewal, reviving its faltering economy and giving it a fresh breath of life. It also began attracting a new set of people from "different shores," making its population ethnically very diverse. The newcomers to Lowell were the refugees from Southeast Asia. These included people from Cambodia, Laos, and Vietnam. Of these the Cambodians were the largest group. In 1981 there were only a few Cambodians in Lowell. However, in three years that number had jumped to 3,000 and was expected to be 5,000 by 1987. Indeed, Lowell became a hub for Cambodian refugees in a matter of a few years after they first started trickling into the city. According to a 1996 report, 40 percent of the Southeast Asian population in Massachusetts consisted of Cambodians,[6] with the majority of these settled in Lowell. In fact, Lowell became the city with the second largest population of Cambodians in the country after Long Beach, California. In the 1990s the *Lowell Sun*, the leading newspaper of Lowell, reported that Cambodians comprised a quarter of the city's population (approximately 25,00 people).[7] However, these numbers that made Lowell the second largest ethnic enclave for Cambodians in the nation are not supported by the 2000 census data. Figure 1 illustrates this. In my own investigation I found the numbers shown in the census data were far below the numbers reported in

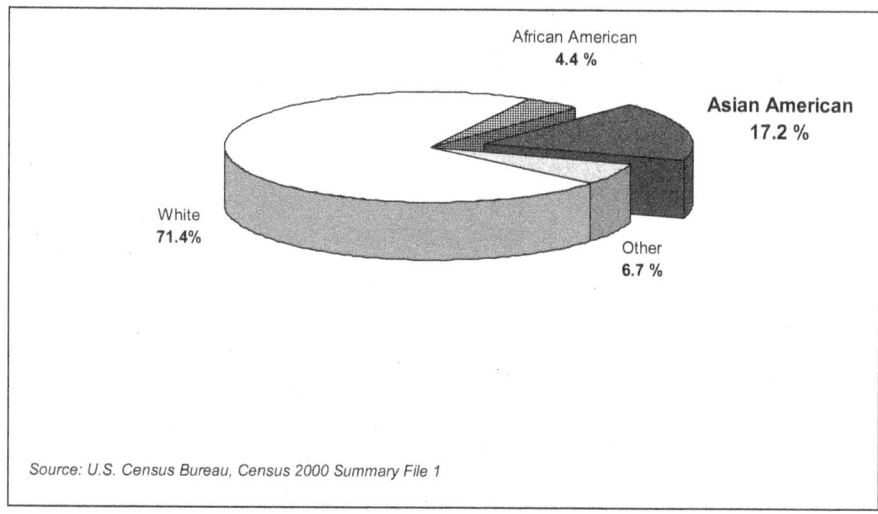

Figure 1. Population of Lowell by Race

the newspaper accounts. However, I was told by one informal source that the actual numbers of people in the city can be gotten by extrapolating the numbers of students in the public school system, assuming each family has five to six members in it. The calculation thus arrived is more in tune with the numbers reported in the media. In the university campus in Lowell where I teach, one can now see many Cambodian students, a visible testimony to their presence in the community.

There were several factors at work in funneling this new group of residents into Lowell. These included new federal laws pertaining to refugees, federal grants and supports channeled through state and local agencies, national and local charity organizations involved with the reception and initial resettlement of refugees coming into the country, and the economic revival of Lowell. Before describing the migration of Cambodians into Lowell, the changes in the laws that allowed the Southeast Asians, specifically the Cambodians, to come and settle in the United States are first described below.

Admission of Refugees

Political developments on the international scene impacted the face of immigrant America here at home. The end of the Vietnam War had created a burgeoning overseas refugee population from Southeast Asian countries. There were refugees from Vietnam, Cambodia, and Laos crowding the refugee camps in the neighboring countries of Thailand and Malaysia. Large numbers of people were fleeing from atrocities, violence, and hunger in Cambodia and crossing the borders into neighboring territories. The influx of refugees into these territories threatened the viability of their own economies. These countries contended that this "problem" thrust upon them with waves of refugees crossing their borders was not of their making and threatened to send refugees back to their home countries. Thailand in the 1980s was reported to have 300,000 Cambodians in their refugee camps.[8] As refugees crossed the Thai border everyday, the refugee problem was getting increasingly worse. Several thousand refugees were indeed sent back, resulting in the deaths of many.[9] Thailand alone is reported to have forcibly sent back 40,000 Cambodian refugees into the mine laden fields of Cambodia where as many as 20,000 people are known to have perished.[10] This incident only illustrated the magnitude of the problem faced by the countries receiving the fleeing refugees.

The inflow of Indochinese refugees into the countries of Southeast Asia put a pressure on the United States to "solve" the refugee problem.[11] The United States and the international community through the United Nations High Commissioner for Refugees had to address the problem of refugee relocation in countries other than the countries of first asylum. Developed countries of the West accepted as many as 1.5 million Southeast Asian refugees between 1975 to 1988, of which, according to one estimate, 829,000 found shelter in the United States. Other developed countries that agreed to take in refugees included Canada, Australia, and France.

Up to this point, the U.S. policy to admit people fleeing persecution in their home countries was confined mainly to communist and fascist regimes. The 1948 Displaced Persons Act was the first expression of the U.S. policy for admitting persons fleeing persecution. Until the late 1950s, refugees admitted to the United States under the provision of this Act were predominantly European in origin. Most of these people came from East European countries under communist governments. When Cubans fleeing Castro's regime were admitted into the United States, this migration pattern was altered. Even so, the refugees still came mainly from the countries of the western hemisphere. It was not until the aftermath of the Vietnam War and the refugee "problem" it created in Southeast Asia that the United States was forced to address this issue of refugee resettlement of the people escaping from countries affected by the war in Southeast Asia.

The period between 1975 to 1979 saw some relief efforts for Southeast Asian refugees due to funds appropriated by Congress for refugee resettlement and admission of IndoChinese refugees under the parole program. But these were far short of the numbers needing assistance. The Cambodian refugees were mainly left out during this time. In 1975, when Pol Pot came to power in Cambodia, there were less than 1,000 Cambodians living in the United States. Due to the tight surveillance of the Khmer Rouge regime, few were able to escape the Cambodian borders, and the news blackout kept the world in the dark as to what was happening within the country. Only with the fall of the Khmer Rouge did large groups of refugees started crossing into neighboring Thailand. It was not until news of the neglect and atrocities against the Cambodian people caught the world's attention that relief for them was made available. Reports and images of people with emaciated bodies in search of food and safety from Thailand made news headlines. President Carter, who was then in office, could no longer remain indifferent to the plight of these new refugees. Before leaving office, Carter's administration agreed to take in 30,000 Cambodian refugees and their claims commenced processing in 1981.[12]

The Congress passed the Refugee Act of 1980 in response to large numbers of people seeking admission in the United States following the end of the Vietnam War. This was a comprehensive and uniform refugee policy enacted with the aim of formalizing the process of refugee admission and resettlement. Its two basic goals were to provide uniform procedures for refugee admission and to provide federal assistance for refugee resettlement.[13] The unique feature of this Act was that for the first time it recognized the right of asylum and the refugee status as a legal category.[14] The Act defined the term *refugee* to conform to the 1967 United Nations Protocol Relating to the Status of Refugees. A refugee is defined as a person outside of his or her country of nationality unable or unwilling to return to that country because of persecution or a well-grounded fear of persecution due to race, religion, nationality, membership in a particular group, or political opinion. In order to be admitted as a refugee in the United States a person had to reside outside of it.

Following the passage of the 1980 Refugee Act, large numbers of Cambodians from Southeast Asia were admitted to this country as refugees on humanitarian grounds. This designation at the time of their entry into the country entitled them to federal aid for resettlement. Refugee resettlement became a thorny issue in the United States as large numbers of Southeast Asians uprooted from their homes and country of origin were admitted as refugees. Many politicians openly opposed an open-door refugee policy. Public opinion polls at that time indicated that people were against massive immigration from Southeast Asia given the sluggishness of the economy and the general prejudice against outsiders who are seen as different. Despite the anti-immigrant sentiment, new programs of resettlement were launched and funds were made available to help Southeast Asian refugees resettle and start a new life in this country. The State Department, through its Office of Refugee Resettlement, and the Department of Health and Human Services were delegated the responsibility of initial reception and resettlement of newly admitted refugees.

The task of resettling refugees involved the efforts of private and public organizations at different levels of the government hierarchy. The money for refugee rehabilitation had to be sanctioned at the federal level and channeled through the state government into the local community. Private voluntary agencies (volags) some of which were religious and others secular, contracted with the Office of Refugee Resettlement of the State Department and received a sum of money for finding sponsors to help resettle refugees. There were sixteen voluntary agencies spread over eleven cities in Massachusetts participating in the Reception and Placement Programs for refugees. The sponsors through whom refugees were resettled could be a person, a group of people, an organization, or a religious institution. The core services that the volags were responsible for started prior to the arrival of refugees: First, they were responsible for identifying individuals or agencies that would assist in refugee sponsorship. Second, upon arrival they had to help the refugees in obtaining the things essential for physical survival such as housing, clothing, food, and furniture for a minimum of thirty days. Third, their responsibilities involved counseling and referral such that refugees could be rehabilitated in the communities of settlement through training and employment that would lead them to independence as early as possible. Several voluntary agencies were involved in Lowell for reception and settlement of refugees. They interfaced with the Department of Health and Human Services (formerly Health, Education and Welfare [HEW]) that worked with the State Department.

The social policy of refugee rehabilitation of the State Department was guided by two considerations. On the one hand, there was concern that the Cuban experience in Miami in the 1960s not be replicated. On the other hand, there was the explicit goal of relocating Cambodians in an orderly manner without much public attention. The task for those responsible for resettlement then was to identify "nonimpacted" areas in the country where newly arriving Cambodians could settle successfully and strengthen ties with existing Cambodian communities in those areas so that the newcomers were provided with an ethnic community support base.[15] The Cambodian Cluster Project, as it was first named, was started in the 1980s to help resettle populations of Cambodians who began arriving in the United States following the Congressional action allowing them to come as refugees to the United States.

Until 1980 a large majority of the 20,000 Cambodians in the country lived in Southern California between Los Angeles and San Diego with Long Beach having as many as 7,000 Cambodians. This region was already inundated with a refugee population and was reportedly inviting anti-refugee protest rumored to take place under the leadership of such groups as the Ku Klux Klan.[16] Therefore, settling any more refugees in that area was considered to be an undesirable option by the State Department and other agencies involved in the refugee resettlement. Other sites had to be found. The Cambodian Association of America scouted for new resettlement sites for their compatriots. States such as Maryland, Massachusetts, Minnesota, Oregon, Texas, West Virginia, in addition to California, became the venues for resettlement for the new refugees to be admitted in the 1980s. The choice for relocation was prompted by such factors as employment opportunities, affordable housing, community support services, and the prevailing atmosphere toward refugees in general in those states.

Once the sites were identified, the associations spearheading the resettlement program entered into negotiations with voluntary agencies at the national level for resettlement of the new incoming refugees from the camps in Thailand or other holding centers. There were thirteen national agencies engaged in resettlement of refugees in the United States. The Office of Refugee Resettlement of the Department of Health and Human Services provided the funds for refugee resettlement programs. Initially, the money allocated for their resettlement was $2,700 per person, later reduced to $1,200. A schedule was worked out by the voluntary agencies to direct the movement of the newly arriving refugees from the camps and centers overseas to the receiving communities here in the United States. Some of these groups even traveled to the refugee camps and the processing centers in Thailand to do orientation and other support work for those included under the Cluster resettlement program. Several church organizations affiliated with some voluntary agencies also sent their personnel to aid in resettlement work. Many refugees converted to Christianity as a means to get early entry into the United States.[17] Of the numbers of Cambodian people admitted in the United States as refugees, the maximum inflow occurred in the ten-year period between 1980 and 1990, the peak being in 1981. This is shown in Figure 2. In 1980 there were approximately 20,000 Cambodians living in the United States. By 1990 their numbers had jumped to 147,000. Thereafter, their numbers dropped, and the inflow of people was reduced to a trickle. According to the 2000 census,

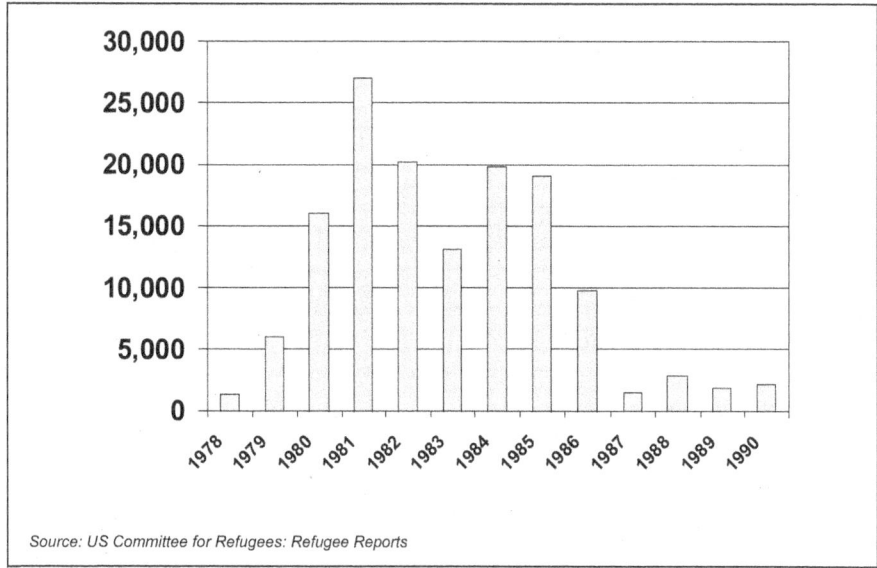

Figure 2. Cambodian Refugees Admitted to the USA

there are 171,937 Cambodians in the United States, part of the 10.2 million Asians in the country, which is approximately 3.6 percent of the total population.[18] The maximum number, totaling a little over 131,000 people, of Cambodian refugees were admitted between the period of 1979 and 1986.[19] Thereafter the numbers started decreasing.

Lowell Receives New Residents

The Cambodians began arriving in Lowell in the 1980s. The first wave of Southeast Asian refugees came to Lowell in the middle of the 1970s, following the end of the war in Vietnam. These consisted mainly of the evacuees from Vietnam. Very few Cambodians and Laotians came at this time. In fact as of early 1970s there were only 300 Cambodians reported to be in the United States.[20] Their inflow gained momentum in the 1980s following the passage of the Refugee Act of 1980 and the publicity of atrocities committed by the Pol Pot regime against its own people. The horrors of the Cambodian revolution described in the previous chapter had precipitated a mass exodus of Cambodians from their land into neighboring countries. There the new arrivals encountered hostility and danger from those who were supposed to protect them. The refugee camps had become temporary waystations for many of the fortunate ones who were able to find sponsors that allowed them to finally leave the refugee camps. Many of those who had been interned in these camps found their way into Lowell. Some came directly from Thailand; others were secondary migrants. The events leading to this process are described below.

The publicity surrounding the migration and plight of refugees into Thailand spurred the quest for refugee resettlement. Massachusetts was identified as one of the states within the country as a place where refugees could be resettled. According to a 1989 demographic report published by the Massachusetts Office of Refugees and Immigrants, approximately 30,000 refugees were admitted to the state since 1975. Between 1978 and 1982 refugee resettlement was the responsibility of volags and their sponsors, since there was no refugee policy within the state under the Republican governor Edward King, who was then in office. The state served as a conduit for federal cash and assistance grants.[21] It was only when Michael Dukakis was elected governor of Massachusetts for the second time following the defeat of his Republican rival that the needs of refugees were addressed. He signed an executive order establishing the Governor's Refugee Advisory Council (GAC). Under his gubernatorial leadership a clear refugee policy sympathetic to the needs of refugee population within the state was promulgated whereby the refugees were entitled to assistance for finding employment placement so that they could be self-reliant. They were also entitled to receive all publicly funded social services as residents of the state. The services of the state agencies that they were entitled to included such agencies as Departments of Welfare, Public Health, Social Services, Mental

Health, Office of Employment and Training, Public Safety, etc.[22] Job opportunities, affordable housing, and public resources for refugee assistance were among the factors that made Massachusetts a favorable place for refugee resettlement—so much so that advocates of the pro-refugee policy in the state faced a stinging criticism by those who were opposed to it.[23]

The first Cambodians arriving in Lowell came directly from the refugee camps and had to be sponsored by an individual or a group to be relocated in this area. Individual Americans as well as private and government agencies provided basic necessities of life and financial and informational support to the refugees they sponsored. Cambodians began to arrive in Lowell as part of the federal refugee resettlement program. The American Fund for Czechoslovak Refugees and the American Council for Nationalities Service were two national organizations involved in the effort to resettle refugees in Lowell. Several local churches and various Mutual Assistance Associations (MAA) such as the Cambodian, Laotian, and the Vietnamese MAAs also provided assistance to the refugees.

Lowell was reported to have 1,400 people of Southeast Asian origin in 1983. By 1990 this number had jumped to 25,000. Of the Southeast Asians residing in Lowell, Cambodians were the largest group, as stated above. As many as 18,000 Cambodians were estimated to reside in Lowell by January 1990. The 2000 Census also reports the Cambodians as the largest group among the Asians in Lowell. This is shown in Figure 3.

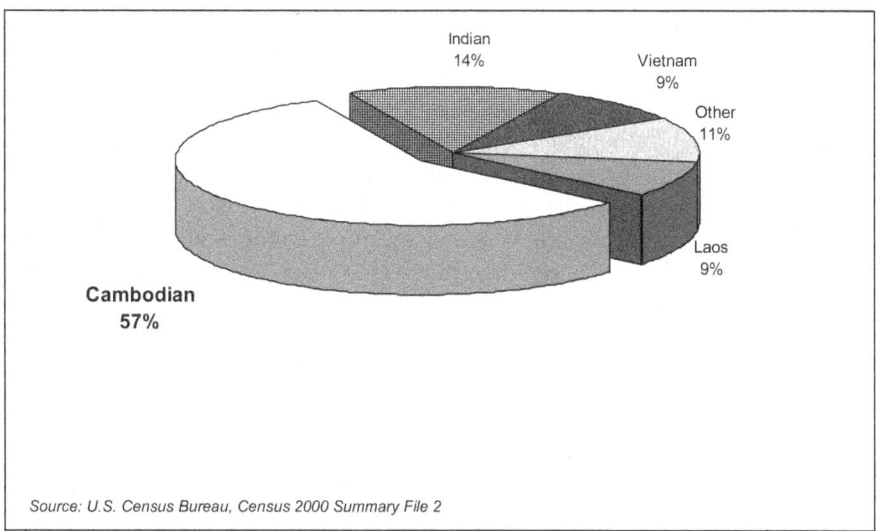

Source: U.S. Census Bureau, Census 2000 Summary File 2

Figure 3. Population by Asian Subgroup in Lowell

Initially the Cambodians who came to Lowell were part of the federally assisted resettlement program. Subsequent numbers to come to Lowell were sponsored by those who were already here and were part of what is known as secondary migration. In the six-year period between 1984 and 1990 a very large number of secondary migrants to Lowell, chiefly Cambodians, inflated the percentage of Southeast Asians to 22 percent of the city's population.[24] Many communities where Southeast Asian refugees were initially settled as part of the federally funded Refugee Resettlement Program migrated to other sites of the country to be close to their relatives and friends. Secondary migration has been an ongoing phenomenon, and large numbers of refugees are reported to have moved to new places across the United States as secondary migrants after having initially settled elsewhere.[25] Several women who participated in this study came to Lowell as secondary migrants. They first arrived in another state and later came to Lowell.

The federally sponsored refugee resettlement program that brought Cambodians into Lowell directly from the refugee camps or processing centers in Southeast Asia allowed the city some leverage over the numbers of people accepted for resettlement in their region. However, once these refugees were settled in the city and were content with their new domicile, they became a magnet for relatives and friends who were dissatisfied with their initial relocation in the country and wanted to move from their place of settlement. The influx of large numbers of secondary migrants was not originally envisioned when Lowell was chosen as a site for refugee resettlement in the early 1980s. As the second wave of refugees started moving into Lowell and became visible because of their numbers, the local residents became resentful of their presence.[26] The city was under pressure for providing a variety of services that it had not planned for. Overcrowding in apartments where more than one family shared the living space was creating a problem of safety (fire hazard) and city officials were known to have discouraged landlords from renting apartments to such families. A Cambodian community leader I had spoken to in the early 1990s complained that the "government was not responding to the needs from below" but dictated what services to provide. The same person went on to state that the schools in the city also were not receptive to the needs of the Cambodian students. The bilingual program that was in place was there "in name only without any curriculum." In fact, a young woman that I interviewed who was part of the program echoed the same sentiment. She was not happy with the bilingual program in her school and complained that separating the Cambodian students from other students worked to their disadvantage as it impeded learning. However, despite the negativity surrounding secondary migrations, many refugees chose the life of "uncertainty with friends and relatives over security with strangers." The *Lowell Sun*, a daily newspaper, reported in March 1988 that the Cambodian population in Lowell was the largest growing population in the city. It reported its population at that time to be 15,000. A large percentage of this population consisted of women and children under the age of eighteen. In fact one estimate indicated that 50 percent of Cambodians in Lowell were below eighteen years old. This was a situation unlike any other immigrant group that came before. Even the Irish women who came to the U.S. in the nineteenth century came as single women with no children as dependents. By contrast, Cambodians who came in the third quarter of the twentieth century consisted of more women with dependent children. The average family size of this group was 5.2, and large numbers of households had four to six children present.[27] It is to such a group of people that Lowell provided a place called home.

Some Examples of Cambodian Migrants to Lowell

The journeys of some of the women interviewed in this study who made it safely to the United States were described in the previous chapter. These women were among the few lucky survivors of a horrible war and were admitted to the United States as refugees. For many, their first destination upon arrival was a state other than Massachusetts. For example, Reasmei and Marina (introduced in the previous chapter) were first settled in Oregon and Maryland, respectively. Mak, by contrast, arrived in Massachusetts with her family—her port of entry was Boston. A relative who lived in a city close to Boston was able to sponsor her along with her siblings with the help of a Catholic charity organization. From there the family moved to Lowell. When she had first moved to Lowell there were only a few Cambodian families and she seemed to have known all of them. Later their numbers had so grown that it was not possible to know everyone. The timing of Mak's arrival suggests that she was part of the initial refugee resettlement program even though she had moved from Boston to Lowell.

Reasmei's family spent a few years in the state of Oregon, where they first settled. Her mother's cousin had sponsored them. They lived with her mother's relative for a month before moving to their separate apartment. Her father found a job that paid minimum wages. It was hard at first. He worried whether he would be able to provide for his family. Her mother also worked in a garment factory sewing clothes. On one occasion her mother visited a relative in Lowell. It was after this visit her mother thought it best for the family to move to Lowell. Moving to Lowell was her mother's decision because she wanted to stay close to her mother (Reasmei's grandmother), who lived in the East Coast. Their first home in Oregon was very modest, and both her parents had to put in long hours of work to make ends meet. Moving to Lowell to be close to family members was a sound decision. It brought many benefits to them as a family. Although they first moved into the area called Acre, they were able to own a house there and settled into a more comfortable home and life than what they had experienced in Oregon. In Lowell, her mother stopped working outside the home. Instead she busied herself with parenting her children and directed some of her energies in family enterprises that earned her some extra household income while being at home. Reasmei emphasized the important role her mother played in her family. She was the authority figure in their household, and even her father always listened to her.

Many of the women interviewed for this study came to Lowell as secondary migrants after first having settled as part of the refugee resettlement program elsewhere. Marina first arrived in Baltimore, Maryland, with her mother and siblings. Her mother's uncle had sponsored her family, including her mother and her siblings. Although her family did not move to Lowell, she did. She came to visit friends in Lowell and eventually settled here after she married a man who was already settled here. Similarly, Savannah, another person interviewed for this study, lived in different places in the United States with her family before she came to Lowell. Upon arrival, she lived in Tennessee for a few years with the family that had sponsored them. From there they moved to Oakland, California, before coming to Lowell. Her mother had relatives in Lowell. Her family was not happy with the environment in California and were particularly concerned about her welfare in a neighborhood that was racially mixed. This may have been a factor in her family's decision to move here. Having relatives already settled here made the decision easier.

Chanti first came to Connecticut from a refugee camp in Vietnam. She worked up to eighteen hours in the refugee camp "just to survive." Life was very difficult in the camp. When she came to this country, she was thirty years old and had three children, the eldest being fourteen years old. She had no relatives in this country. She was a single parent, and it was hard raising three children all by herself. It was later that her husband joined her in Connecticut. It was from Connecticut that they moved to Lowell. Their decision to move to Lowell was prompted by personal and business interests. Her husband was interested in starting his own business, and if it was successful, she and her husband planned to eventually move back to Cambodia. The absence of ethnic institutions in Connecticut may have provided Chanti and her husband an added incentive to come to Lowell. She stated that she and her husband were not young any more and would like to enjoy life. When they first came to Lowell on a visit, they went to eat at a Cambodian restaurant, as there were no such restaurants in Connecticut. In Lowell they found they could pursue business interests and also enjoy some of the things that suited their tastes.

Among the factors underlying secondary migration, the presence of family and friends who belonged to the same ethnic group played a key role in the decision of these refugees to come to Lowell and settle here. Migration in general is a kin-driven process. Initial settlers of family and friends serve as a line of defense and support to migrants who come later. They are able to provide material and informational support that can be valuable to the newcomers; they can also act as counselors to those who come after them, giving them the benefit of their own experience and knowledge. If one examines the migration and settlement patterns of immigrants and refugees coming into this country, one is likely to find that "settlement decisions are affected by ethnic concentrations established by compatriots in the past."[28] It is not an accident that new arrivals gravitate toward already-established ethnic communities. This was so in the past and it is still true. In the 19th century when Lowell was a developing industrial economy, kinship relations were used to recruit, place, and settle friends and family in textile factories of Lowell. The Irish and subsequent ethnic groups that came to Lowell followed the same kin route to settlement. More recently, the Southeast Asian refugees have used kinship lines to move to areas that have concentrations of their compatriots. The role of kinship in secondary migration has been documented extensively.[29] Among Southeast Asians the use of fictive kinship relations in the absence of real kinship relationships to migrate to areas with strong Southeast Asian concentration has been noted.[30] In a country culturally and linguistically different, people sharing the same ethnic background may provide a degree of security and comfort that may explain why large numbers of refugees move to areas to join family and friends from the area of initial relocation. This in itself may be important in the process of resettlement.

The Cambodian community is the largest of the Southeast Asian groups settled in Lowell. The Laotians and the Vietnamese communities, the other two Southeast Asian groups, are much smaller by comparison. The influx of Cambodian refugees in Lowell since the mid-1980s has led to dramatic changes in the city. The housing pattern, the schools, and the business environment have all been affected.[31] Nancy Costello, a reporter with *Lowell Sun* that I had spoken to in the mid 1990s had suggested that in the next ten years the Southeast Asians would be an influential community within the city from the trends discernible. The numbers of businesses that have opened up in Lowell owned and operated by Southeast Asians, especially Cambodians, seems to validate her prediction. A recent news article reported in the *Lowell Sun* indicated that the growth of immigrant population in the state has helped the economy by its labor force participation. Lowell was cited for the growth of its immigrant population. "These new immigrants are important assets for the Commonwealth's economy,"[32] although there is a need for increased training and education so that these people can better participate in the state's economy.

The Cambodians are one of the newest Asian groups to arrive on the scene. Their stories of migration and incorporation into American society are in many ways different from other Asian groups who came before them with a different legal status. In some ways, the social traits manifested by this group account for this difference. Indeed, the incoming groups of refugees have differed from each other, depending on the timing of their entry. Refugees who came to the United States in the first and second waves of migration after 1975 were better off compared to the bulk of the Cambodians who came in the third wave. The latter were less educated, principally from rural backgrounds, much younger in age, and as such not equipped with the skills needed to survive in a modern urban environment, although before coming to this country many took English classes and were given instruction about Western etiquette and other information essential for everyday life experience in the country that sponsored them. Still, for many it was like a leap in time. Eventually, of course, people adapt to the environment in which they are placed in ways they know how. However, their adaptation is nevertheless influenced and shaped by the cultural, social, and economic conditions associated with their lives. Migration can be problematic if the incoming groups lack the necessary education and other social skills that can be traded in the market. How these factors shape the process of adaptation in American society and economy is the issue that we turn to in the chapter that follows.

CHAPTER FOUR

A New Beginning: Challenges and Opportunities

The city of Lowell is an ethnic laboratory. Many new migrants began their journeys here on the road to settlement in the United States. Large numbers of the Cambodian refugees are beginning to make their presence visible in Lowell. As one drives into the area leading to the South Campus of the University of Massachusetts, one can hardly ignore the variety of Southeast Asian shops with inscriptions written in Khmer along with English signs describing the nature of the product or service the store sells. Driving along the same route early in the morning one can also see Cambodian children and adults waiting for the school bus in the morning. These are signs of settlement. A large number of these residents who have settled in Lowell are of foreign origin. This is supported by the census data. The 1990 census data reports that of all the Asian residents of Lowell, 80 percent were foreign born.[1] According to the 2000 census, of the total population of 105,167 people in Lowell, 22.1 percent of people are foreign born.[2] This number is significantly larger compared to the proportion of foreign-born people living in the neighboring towns surrounding Lowell. The percentage of foreign-born people in Lowell and surrounding towns is shown in Map 3.

Despite Lowell's reputation as an immigrant friendly city, its new residents have had to deal with problems that migration to a new land may entail. Migration to a new land can be difficult even when it is voluntary. However, when people are forced to leave their country of domicile due to circumstances beyond their control, relocation can be a bumpy process. Refugees fleeing countries plagued with internecine conflicts are faced with different prospects and problems than those migrants who come as immigrants

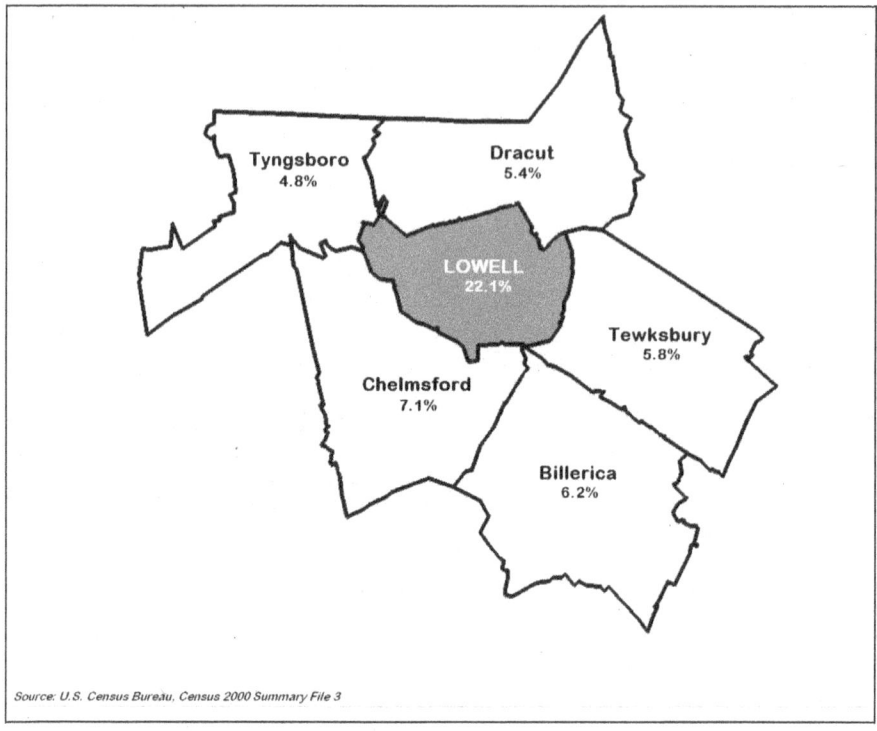

Map 3. Foreign-Born Population in Lowell and Surrounding Communities

in pursuit of better life chances. As refugees, the Cambodians were victims of war and violent repression in their country. Their experiences of terror and violence have affected their psychological and mental health, and many refugees have noted how they are never likely to forget it. But they are also survivors who successfully escaped the ravages of war to find refuge in this country. As such, their situation represents a different social and political reality compared to individuals admitted to this country as legal immigrants. The refugee status of Cambodians entitled them to public assistance not available to immigrants. Indeed, between the periods of 1975 to 1986, the United States government is reported to have spent some $5 billion in cash and other forms of assistance to refugees from that region of the world. This aid was much needed and helped many refugees to meet their minimal survival needs. One twenty-three-year-old woman, who was two years old when she first came to this country, acknowledged that her family survived because they received welfare. Her mother she said "still had to work to make ends meet," and when she was around five years old she was called upon to assist her mother in household chores so that her mother could work at "odd hours." She recalled that at five years of age she had begun to "stir fry" and do other odd jobs around the house, and by the time she was thirteen she had started to work an assembly line job to supplement her family income (she looked older than her thirteen years and was able to work). Other women in my study have also alluded to the government assistance they received as refugees that allowed them to establish separate residences after first spending some time in the household of their sponsors. The public assistance, although important for their survival, was bare minimum and needed to be supplemented with other incomes. So even with cash assistance, the incorporation and resettlement of Cambodian refugees into American society has been a complex process accompanied by many unanticipated and unintended consequences.

A large number of Asian immigrants, who came to the U.S. in pursuit of economic and professional opportunities, were educated with skills to operate in the U.S. economy. According to the 1990 Census, more than a third of the Asian immigrants who came to this country between 1980 to 1990 had completed college education. According to recent census data, of the 28 million foreign-born persons residing in the United States, 26 percent were born in Asia. The majority of the Asian immigrants had college degrees and fall under some skilled labor category. Although there are regional variations in the percentage of college graduates among Asians, 45 percent of the college-educated immigrant workforce is Asian.[3] As noted elsewhere,[4] contrary to popular beliefs, people who migrate beyond the boundaries of their nations are not the most impoverished and abject poor but are people with informational and other resources that allow them to find well-paid jobs. Cambodians (also from an Asian country) came here not out of choice but out of the need of sheer physical survival.

As stated above, Cambodians had no control over the circumstances that drove them out of their homeland. They would not have come to this country if their world had not been so shaken up by the political events that traumatized their country. They had not planned to come to this country, and vast numbers of them had minimal or no school education. As such, the issues they were faced with upon arrival and their patterns of adaptation are somewhat different. If one examines the social and economic background of the Cambodian refugees, most of them came from very rural backgrounds, had very little formal education, and consisted of a much younger population. Their median age is reported to be less than 20.[5] According to the 2000 Census, 44 percent of Cambodians in Lowell are under the age of eighteen.[6] In central part of the city that has a large Cambodian population, poverty is prevalent. The median income is $10,000, and many households are female headed with very low educational levels.[7] As noted earlier, a large number of Cambodian refugees were single woman with young children, their husbands having been killed by the Pol Pot soldiers. These conditions alone provide for a differential social context within which resettlement took place and must be taken into account in the strategies and issues that emerged in their lives.

Challenges of Migration

Moving to a new country is not easy even with elaborate preparation. I came to this country as a student wife married to a graduate student already here in the United States. Upon arrival, we found that we did not have a place to live (the housing arrangements my husband had made prior to our arrival fell through). We spent some difficult days until we found our own affordable place. However, we were connected to the university student community that was our source of information of where to look for help; most importantly, we were both educated and could speak English. But when foreigners (whether immigrants or refugees) are new to a country—and more importantly are also lacking significant language and economic skills that can be a passport to"making it in America"—the situation is very different and problematic. The women in my study expressed relief and gratitude in having the chance to escape the horrors of war and get a second chance in life. They wanted to forget the horrible experiences they endured in the labor camps of their home country. However, the road to resettlement in the United States has not been uniform for all refugees admitted to this country. Some have made a new beginning and found liberty and opportunities for a successful life, while others have been stymied by their presence here. These differential experiences are associated with their individual and group traits. Adaptation and subsequent assimilation is both an individual and a collective process wherein the individuals and the recipient host society are interlocked in determining the outcomes of the process of adaptation. A parent liaison worker with the Lowell School Department noted that the difference between those who make it without government assistance and those who don't rests on the combination of factors such as length of time in this country, education, and personality.[8] To these others factors can be added. The new immigrant community itself can be a source of strength, although it may present challenges of its own. These will be elaborated in greater detail in the pages that follow.

From Third-World Citizen to First-World Refugee

For many Cambodians coming to America was also like making a journey through time into a completely alien and unknown situation. A leader of the Cambodian Mutual Assistance Association (CMAA) that I interviewed[9] when I first started this research expressed it best, when he stated that the people of the third world (referring to refugees from his country) have a mindset that is unequipped to function in the first world. He spoke of the refugees being "so far behind" that it is "hard to catch up." By coming to the United States refugees were "making a big leap in time." It was both a temporal and a spatial jump for them. From very rural and simple backgrounds suddenly they had to deal with problems of survival in a very different cultural and spatial set up. At least one woman that I interviewed had not heard of the United States, knew nothing about this country, and had no idea of what she was coming to. Many refugees had not planned to come to the United States when they escaped to Thailand. They were in the camps to get away from the fighting that was surrounding their country. It was only in the refugee camps they first discovered that many of their relatives had come to the United States.[10] Indeed, one woman I had interviewed said she did not even know this country was her final destination until she boarded the plane. Others wanted to come to the U.S. having heard about it from their relatives here who had come before them. Samy (mentioned earlier) thought of the U.S. as heaven and was happy about her admission to the U.S. Some refugees came to Lowell directly from the camps of Thailand. Others are secondary migrants.[11]

Lowell acted as a magnet for refugees for several reasons. Among these were the presence of previously settled kin, the information regarding economic opportunities, the availability of social services, and the presence of a Buddhist temple built in the vicinity of Lowell.[12] A seventy-nine-year-old woman I spoke to was very happy to be in Lowell because of the temple she found here. She went to it each day and spent some time there. Regardless, the conditions that prompted the refugees to leave their homes and homeland were painful, and refugees eagerly sought to leave them behind. It was part of their life history they wanted to forget and yet could not. Samy mentioned earlier said she would never forget how "crazy and horrible" the communists were. "It was just awful" she said. Another woman who has done a lot of volunteer work in the community impressing teenagers of the importance of education and how it can open windows of opportunities stated that she remembers the agony of losing a sibling to starvation. She feels that she has to succeed not only for herself but also for the sake of her sibling so that this death was not in vain. Many women felt that in coming to this country, they got the opportunity to make a new beginning.[13] They invested their energies and efforts into starting a new life in a land that was now their home. Some have succeeded and others are still struggling.

Minor Challenges

The road to resettlement in America (and Lowell) included both major and minor problems not envisioned earlier. Some of these caught the newcomers unprepared. The difference in food habits and taste is an example of a minor difficulty. Reasmei, described earlier, was a twenty-two-year-old senior in college when I interviewed her. She laughed when she mentioned how food was a problem when she first arrived here in the United States. It not only tasted different; it was not satisfying either. "Sandwiches do not fill you up like rice," she said. Cambodian food has more bulk, although fewer calories compared to Western food. That may be a reason for not feeling filled. In a culture where eating rice is viewed as part of one's well-being and "Have you eaten rice?" is used as a form of greeting, this is understandable.[14] Some refugees reported they were hungry in a land where food was abundant due to their inability to ingest U.S. food, such as cans of Campbell® soup. There were also newspaper reports of clothing and attire being problems for refugees unused to the cold winter in the Northeast. Recently arrived Cambodian people were seen walking in the snow wearing flip-flops. Learning rules of etiquette and modifying behavior also posed challenges. It was only after being rebuked for breaking the line that a young woman learned that one had to wait for one's turn rather than "shove with one's elbow" to "get ahead" in order to be served.

A woman affiliated with a church in Lowell involved in resettlement of Cambodians in the city had some interesting insights to offer. She was also a sponsor for some refugees. She recalled with amusement the excitement of the refugees in her charge when they were shown an apartment with basic kitchen appliances and minimal furniture that they could move into. She was referring to their simple backgrounds unaccustomed to the furniture and appliances of a modern home. In a rural setup in Cambodia there is one large central room for living, eating, and sleeping; meals are taken on a mat, and furniture is very meager.[15] So homes in an urban center of the United States are very different by comparison. However, learning to handle modern kitchen appliances and sleeping on mattresses is not the difficult part. These examples, embarrassing or uncomfortable they may have been initially, are minor challenges that are soon overcome. Challenges and difficulties that result in serious disadvantages in resettlement and adaptation in the United States may have less to do with habits and cultural styles than with attributes and qualifications (social and human capital) that are known to be useful in the process of assimilation. These are elaborated below.

The Language Problem

The most difficult problem faced by many Cambodians is the language problem. Even those who have come to this country with some working knowledge of English may find themselves at a loss by the way English is spoken here, with its accent and different cultural expressions. I have known some very smart people with speaking competency in English who have not gotten positions commensurate with their qualifications because of their accents. I learned English when I was five years old, and I was educated in a very British school in India; yet I found it difficult to understand a particular professor who spoke with a strong American accent. I remember the frustration I felt at my inability to comprehend him, and at one time felt that this might prevent me from successfully completing my graduate studies in the U.S. For Cambodian women with little or no knowledge of English, the problem is far more serious than mere comprehension. It is a matter of survival, the ability to access basic opportunities of economic independence and self-sufficiency. The problem is particularly serious among those who are not so young and have had no exposure to any kind of education. I was told by a woman who works in an organization that provides nutritional help to infants, children, and women that many Cambodian women who seek help at that agency do not speak any English at all. Some of these women are completely illiterate. They cannot even read Khmer, their native language. For such people, learning of English seems to be a formidable task. A former U.S. student of mine who has worked with multilingual people corroborates this. She noted that non-English-speaking European and South/Central Americans who spoke such languages as French or Spanish had an easier time learning English than such people as the Cambodian or the Chinese. The European languages share the same structural elements "such as inflections, articles, tenses and letter coding." Khmer and Chinese, on the other hand "hardly use inflection or tense in their language system." These people have a harder time adapting to a different "decoding and phonetic system,"[16] and consequently struggle with English. One refugee woman (Sokha) stated learning English was difficult for her. This problem of learning English by refugees has been explained as the result of their inability to "understand things like past tense, present tense, and future tense."[17] And without the rudimentary language skills, these people are severely disadvantaged. Sokha noted that she wants to work but finds it difficult to get a job without the knowledge of English.

Sokha, a middle-aged woman in her late forties when I interviewed her, acknowledged the difficulty she experienced in learning the English language. Her husband, who was several years older, could not find work due to his language deficiency. Even after attending classes for adult learners, she and her husband had no success. Such people find themselves isolated and excluded from even minimal economic and social opportunities. "Who would hire them? Where could they work?" she and her husband asked me. This couple showed visible signs of despair and helplessness. And with the talk of an impending federal proposal to deny welfare benefits to non-citizens, the situation for them seemed very dire indeed. Another woman I interviewed was thirty-seven years old and employed in a factory that manufactured medical instruments. She worked in an assembly line job and felt that even though the quality of her work was good and her boss appreciated her work, her opportunities for advancement were restricted. Although her job was permanent, she could not move up the ladder because of her inability to speak English fluently. Her pay was "okay not good," she said. Although her situation was much better than the woman mentioned before her, her prospects of earning a living commensurate with her skills would have been greater with better communication skills in English.

Even people who are born and have grown up in this country find themselves handicapped if they do not speak English correctly and properly. Employers are reluctant to employ such people because of their lack of proper language skill.[18] Several years ago when it was suggested that Ebonics (Black English) be introduced in schools in California, there were some prominent

African Americans who opposed the move on the ground that learning proper English is imperative if one has to operate in today's economy. The knowledge of English as a first step to avail the advantages of this "land of opportunity" has been acknowledged and documented in a variety of popular and scholarly writings. Of all the Asian immigrants in this country who have come in the thirty-year period between 1970 to 2000, the groups that top the list in terms of median income earnings are also those who have the highest levels of college graduates. These include the East Indians (South Asians). The Cambodian refugees, by contrast, because of their strong rural origins with limited educational opportunities, had much smaller numbers of people with high school education. The bulk of their numbers had less than elementary education. The 2000 Census reported that among the Southeast Asians, of which the Cambodians are the largest group, there is a severe problem with English language.[19] Over three-quarters of Cambodians 65 years or older speak English "not well or not at all" and over one-third of working-age Cambodians report a similar lack of English proficiency.[20] Even those Southeast Asian children who are born in this country have difficulty with English language when they first arrive at school.[21]

Inability to speak English handicaps both women and men. But the issue of language becomes women's issue when one considers the rates of illiteracy among the Cambodians. According to a United Nations Human Development Report, Cambodian women get only 1.7 years of education during their lifetime.[22] Another source reports more than 50 percent of Cambodian women are illiterate, compared to only 20 percent of Cambodian men.[23] These numbers indicate the status of Cambodian women compared to Cambodian men. More recent figures from official sources also support the poor levels of educational attainments among Cambodians, especially Cambodian females.[24] The problems associated with illiteracy and lack of effective language skills for women are not economic alone. Their ability to effective familial and parenting roles also is affected. We shall turn to this later.

Importance of Education

Learning of English in particular and getting an education in general are critical for economic survival in this country. This is well understood and recognized by all the women I talked to in this study. One has to "earn money in order to survive here" was an opinion expressed frequently. This opinion probably reflects the rural background of the many women who grew up in Cambodia. Cambodia was basically an agricultural society and large numbers of people, as noted in Chapter Two, lived in villages where the economy was subsistence based. Food was not bought in stores; rather, it was domestically grown on one's own plot for familial consumption. Earning of money was not critical for one's survival. However, in a wage-based economy such as the United States, money is an important resource. It determines one's quality of life. Therefore, the importance of education for accessing opportunities for economic success and material welfare is recognized by parents and emphasized to their children. Indeed, many Cambodian children are known to excel in their educational programs.[25] All the women interviewed in this study recognized the importance of education for economic success. Because they appreciate its value, some of them are pursuing a college degree in the night school in the hope of increasing their economic potential. Even Sokha, who was unable to learn English (mentioned earlier), expected her eldest child, a daughter who was in high school, to finish school and go on for higher education. Indeed, all of them valued education and considered the availability of universal education for all children a very desirable aspect of American society. Some of the younger women in my study who came to this country as children had finished their college education here; others had high school education. Some older women I had interviewed had young children. Those who had gone through schooling here and had some level of competence that allowed them access to jobs seemed to express confidence in themselves and what they could do with their lives. They also recognized the importance of education for making it in America. Almost unanimously the women I interviewed reported how happy they were because their children had the opportunity to go to school here. Similar sentiments have been reported in other ethnographic accounts of Cambodian refugees. If one looks at the demographic figures of number of children in the public school system from the time that Lowell started receiving refugees in the 1980s to present times, one can see the high numbers of Cambodian children in the public schools. According to figures reported in the *Lowell Sun*, Cambodian students comprised the largest percent of minority students in Lowell public schools. Of the 46 percent minority students, 26 percent were Asians. Among the Asians, Cambodians are the largest group in Lowell.[26] Phala Chea, coordinator of the Parent Information Center of the Lowell Public Schools, suggested that her "educated guess" was that of the Asians in the public schools in Lowell 85 percent were Cambodians.[27]

Language and Power Relationship Changes

Women with children, regardless of their age, aspired for educational success of their children, not unlike their Asian counterparts. However, they also seemed to be concerned as parents about protecting their children from educational derailment given the abundant opportunities this society provides for courses of action that challenge parental authority. Repeatedly, I heard from women how difficult it is to raise children in America. Women complained of excessive freedom given to children in this country, and this is an aspect of American society many did not like. This concern with excessive freedom is understandable in view of the highly publicized problems of gangs and teenage sexual activity reported in the newspapers that plague the Cambodian community in such alarming proportions.[28] All the women I interviewed who had children were concerned about these problems. Sokha (cited above) stated that American society gives too many rights to children. This is the reason why "kids are bad" and join gangs. "They don't listen to their parents, threaten them, refer to the law." She has seen that happen. In their homeland, children listened to their parents and obeyed them. Parents had the absolute power, authority, and control over their children. And the society at large morally and institutionally supported them. In the United States, many parents, particularly those without English language competency, depend upon their children to interface with the larger society and in so doing lose leverage over their children. A student of mine who worked in a juvenile program informed me that some children misuse their knowledge of English, keep parents in the dark about their activities and sometimes get into trouble with the law. When children are a conduit for their parents to the outside world, the power relation in the family changes. A child's fluency in English turns "family relationship on its head." Parents become dependent upon their children, and this role reversal leaves "parents feeling impotent and children overly anxious."[29] Children soon realize their own strength and the vulnerability of their own parents. Without appropriate language skill, parents lose control over their children. The situation is further aggravated because of the cultural divide that separates the parents from their children. Traditional parenting styles do not permit any dialogue across generations. Parents and children "often find it difficult to communicate because they realize they have very different conceptions of healthy parent/child relationships."[30] Consequently, there is no meaningful communication between them. Further, because of their need to earn incomes and work schedules, many parents are unable to supervise their children after school hours.

Several parents expressed their dissatisfaction with the policy of the state to interfere with parental jurisdiction. While they could not do anything about it, they felt that their rights to parental discipline were encroached upon. One woman who worked in a social service agency had run into disfavor with her community because of her espousal of a child's rights. She saw what was considered to be acceptable behavior by the family of the child as abuse. And when she wanted to help the child, she was criticized for her intervention.

Between Two Worlds

The above illustrations indicate that the process of adaptation of Cambodian immigrants into the American cultural fabric is not smooth, uniform, or conflict free. While some norms are adopted without any problem, others are met with resistance and even rejection. The importance of education as a gateway to a better life is accepted by adults and impressed upon children. But education is also a double-edged sword. While it enhances the adaptability of children of immigrants or refugees to American society and culture by providing them with needed skills and knowledge, it also is a vehicle for internalizing powerful cultural messages that form the bulwark of the American cultural script. In schools children learn about individualism, independence, and the right to express their opinions. These cultural messages permeate the society at large and are also reinforced by other societal institutions. These afford individuals with opportunities for behaviors that threaten the fundamental premises of the immigrant culture. This is demonstrated when individuals want to pursue behavioral choices considered traditionally unacceptable in Cambodian culture. Essentially, the problem is caused by a clash of two dissimilar cultural systems juxtaposed together.

The idea of individual freedom and personal happiness are important cultural ideals in U.S. society. In Cambodian culture, submitting to the wishes and deference to elders and subordination of the individual for the welfare of the group is emphasized. As Sarika pointed out, Cambodian children are expected to be "reserved and not talk back." Girls in particular should "play the Cambodian role" by keeping quiet rather than speaking up. The U.S. cultural ideals emphasize personal liberty and pursuit of happiness. These are very attractive to individuals growing up in this society. But they also present a challenge to the preceding generation of adults who are interested in having their children abide by their wishes. Parents are concerned with "orderly replacement" of cultural and familial forms in the next generation. Only then can they successfully replicate their cultural ways into the next generation of their children. This exposure to conflicting value systems, one at home and the other in the society at large, puts children and adults alike in a very difficult situation. Both are faced with challenges. Anny, an eleven-year-old girl at school in Lowell, behaves in ways commensurate with children her age. However, when she comes home, she is expected to be a "true daughter of Cambodia" and act in ways that her mother wants her to. "A free-thinking girl could upset the delicate system of checks and balance of family life."[31] Cultural conflict involved in such situations sometimes leads to actions where children are forced to conform to parental wishes that can end their personal aspirations. For example, I have heard of girls being forced to marry individuals selected for them by their parents to ward off the possibility of self-selection of mates or engaging in behaviors that will put the family to shame. In one particular instance, a promising career never got off to a start. The girl in question was academically very bright and might have excelled in college. But she never got that chance. She was married off soon after matriculation from high school and settled down to a life of homemaker and a mother. A community volunteer worker involved with troubled Cambodian youth in the community indicated that many parents do not support higher education for girls. Sarika, a young woman I interviewed, was a teenager in high school when she was married to a Cambodian boy. Her older sister arranged her marriage. This was done to protect her from the problems that many girls her age were seen to fall prey to such as early initiation into sexual activity, pregnancy, or running away from home to avoid parental discipline. Sarika was twenty years old when I interviewed her. At that time she was already a mother of a four-year-old son. She had separated from her husband. Unwilling to be put in a traditional mold of servitude in her husband's home, she ended her marriage, even though it meant being a single mother at a very young age. I have been told that many girls elope with their boyfriends to escape parental disapproval of their spousal choices. At a conference on refugees that I recently attended, a participant noted that many girls between the ages of fourteen to sixteen run away from home to be with their boyfriends.[32] Sarika, for instance, was married at the age of fourteen to prevent her from running away from home.

The force of tradition is disproportionately exerted on girls by their parents. Boys are given a lot more leeway. A young woman, a community activist I spoke to, reported that if girls deviate from the expected gender norms considered appropriate for girls, they are looked upon negatively and labeled *hok-lote*. She mentioned she had been so labeled by her father, who did not approve of her ways. Her sister left home after graduating from college and came to live with her because her parents disapproved of her having male friends. Chanda, a thirty seven-year-old woman who had two daughters, did not allow her children any freedom to go out with friends after school to parks or shopping malls because of her fear of the perils of adolescent freedom. She said that only when they were in their early twenties would she allow them to go out unchaperoned. Reasmei, mentioned earlier, also reported of the strict discipline of her mother at home. Growing up she was never allowed to go out with her friends to the mall or movies like many American girls her age are accustomed to doing. That girls are not allowed to do the things that American adolescents experience normally has been suggested by others involved with the resettlement process.[33]

Examples cited above illustrate the pressure and conflict that adolescent and young girls face while growing up in the United States. Their parents, like many immigrant parents before them, want them to carry on their ethnic cultural traditions and are opposed to adoption of American ways of behaving. Heterosexual mixing of the sexes prior to marriage is one of the issues that many first-generation newcomers have been opposed to. Of course, many children also challenge the authority of their parents. And this has been possible because in this society freedom and rights of the individual are accepted as fundamental cultural norms and values. In Cambodia, by contrast, parents had authority over their children and could compel them to obey. Transgression of rules could evoke corporal punishment to compel compliance to parental wishes.[34] These examples illustrate the difficulty inherent in traversing between two distinct cultural roadways particularly for children who are growing up in America. For individuals who find themselves in situations noted above, it must be agonizing to be torn between tradition and change. Many teenagers have indicated that they find their parents too strict and old-fashioned. This is an issue wherein two generations of individuals within a family from different cultural perspectives are juxtaposed together. It leads to a struggle between opposing forces: continuing tradition versus adopting change. That this is an issue that the community is confronting is evident from the newspaper accounts covering the cultural conflict between generations of Cambodian parents and their children. A Lowell newspaper reported that a group leader under the auspices of the Cambodian Mutual Assistance Association (CMAA) has attempted to teach Cambodian girls how to cope with growing up in America where being American and Cambodian is not mutually exclusive.[35] CMAA Youth Corps members, including several teenagers who experienced difficulties themselves, are taking the initiative to help and listen to their peers who are caught up in "culture wars" at home. In a conference organized in Boston in December 1993 more than 600 students from eastern Massachusetts, including many from Lowell, gathered to share their struggles as young Asian Americans trying to adapt to U.S. society. Such topics as youth-parent relationships, interracial dating, prejudice, and other problems related to Asian youths were under discussion to allow the participants to explore ways by which a balance and harmony can be reached between American and the homeland cultures of the refugees. Other conferences dealing with these issues have been organized in subsequent years, including one in 2004. This is an important community issue. Unless addressed and resolved, its ramifications are far more serious where the entire city is impacted by its problems seen in such things as school dropout and runaway kids, gang membership, premarital pregnancy, etc. For newcomers (refugees and immigrants) adaptation is as much a function of social groups as it is of individuals, and the ethnic group plays a key role in the process. Newcomers with cultural and language barriers are likely to be at a disadvantage in finding solutions to their problems due to either lack of information or the inability to access resources that would redress their difficulties. Cultural as well as societal factors have created problems of adaptation for these new residents of the city. Some of the community leaders I spoke to have underscored this fact also.

Thus far I have tried to underscore the cultural difficulties inherent in the process of adaptation among the Cambodians who have settled here. Some of these difficulties are not unique to them alone. Immigrants of other nationalities also encounter difficulties when children come of age and want to follow cultural scripts popular here but unacceptable to their parents. I know that many Indian parents who have adolescent or older children find themselves in a cultural fix. While they want their children to economically succeed and enjoy the material prosperity that the United States offers, they also want them to remain "Indian" and adhere to their traditional cultural rules and values. This is especially expected of girls. A woman's organization, Saheli, conducted workshops recently[36] to address some of the issues that Asian Indian children are experiencing as they are sandwiched between the norms of their parents, their own needs and wishes, and the influences and forces that they have absorbed living in this society.

In the Cambodian community some of these problems are magnified and are far more publicized than what has been the case in other communities. The gang problem and the problem of teenage pregnancy that one frequently hears about are examples of problems confronting the Cambodian community.[37] Almost all the women I talked with mentioned the presence of these problems in their community. Chanda, noted above, controlled the movement of her daughters because of the fear of the dangers that lurked in the community. She did not allow her daughters to hang out with friends. She took them with her everywhere she went. Even so, she was not fully able to insulate her children from the forces operating in society at large. Her younger daughter became pregnant and gave birth to a child out of wedlock. Similarly, Sarai, who had a college degree in psychology, decided to defer seeking employment to be with her two young sons because of the problems she saw around her. Both of these women took actions they thought were in the best interest of their children. Their actions were geared toward avoiding the problems that they saw many around them succumbing to. When large numbers of children in a community are experiencing difficulties resulting in problems that spill beyond the boundaries of the home, then the problem is not personal. It is a social problem. The conditions that give rise to it may be inherent in the structures of social relations present in this community. One can assume that enforcement of traditional Khmer norms on children who are basically growing up in the United States is likely to be difficult if the society at large does not support these rules. A woman who was involved with the community affairs in the CMAA told me that the children disobey their parents here because they (the children) had not been a part of the Cambodian culture their parents wanted them to abide by. These children had not seen Cambodian culture in action because they essentially are growing up in this society. This may be part of the reason of the chasm that divides the parents and their children.

The importance of social and economic background of families, however, cannot be discounted in examining these problems. Children of women with poor social and economic backgrounds are likely to be more prone to greater risk compared to children from informed and more educated families. The women in my study who had successfully completed their educational goals and were holding respectful jobs had parents who were able to help them achieve their goals. Lan Pho noted that when parents set high educational and career goals for their children, the children do better than those whose parents don't set such goals. Also children who enjoy a satisfactory or positive relationship with their parents perform better in schools.[38]

Economic factors can affect the process of adaptation. The ability to access economic opportunities can pave the way for social and cultural adjustments or at least reduce the impact of cultural conflict. This is seen in the lives of the women I interviewed. I am reminded of Aam, who was in her late forties. She was the mother of three children. When I interviewed her, she was at home full time. Her husband was the principal economic provider in her family. She also earned some income through investments in businesses that she could manage from the home. She provided child-care services and rented out some property she owned. She had worked after coming to this country in order to make ends meet. But now that her husband was settled with a stable income, she did not work outside the home so that she could take care of her children. She kept a tight control over her children's social activities outside of school. She believed that children could do "bad things" and get in "trouble" if parents were not strict with them. It was her concern about the problems that many children get into that she monitored the activities of her children after school. She said that she provided her children with all the things they need so that they cannot complain or be lured into undesirable activities. Her older daughter, a senior in college, was given a car for her use. In exchange, Aam got her children to act in culturally appropriate ways. None of her children had friends of the opposite sex or went out dating with them. Her younger daughter, with whom I had spoken when I visited them, was not happy with her mother for not allowing her to do the things normal for her peers. The strict home environment does not indicate absence of love and affection or parental guidance. On the contrary, it was Aam's love for her children that prompted her to remain at home so that she could attend to their needs. Of course, she had the benefit of a stable comfortable family income to provide her children with all the material amenities they needed while she also supervised and guided them. She was in charge of running and managing the household, including the activities of her children. It was her economic situation that allowed her to dictate the terms of parental control over her children's activities.

The debate of culture versus structure is not a new one in sociology. Proponents and opponents have argued over the importance of culture (values) or structure (opportunities) in explaining the problems afflicting groups or individuals. Adaptation is a multidimensional process, and whether an individual or a family is successful ultimately depends upon resources that members can access.

Opportunities and challenges are not mutually exclusive. Opportunities bring new challenges. Some victories may involve some losses, too. The women I interviewed exemplify this through their life course. Cambodian culture rooted in Buddhist values is hierarchical. Status inequality between parents and children, husbands and wives, is institutionalized and normative. This is to say that cultural norms confer legitimacy to such status distinctions. A Cambodian woman who helped me interview non-English speaking Khmer women surprised and confused me with two of her comments about Cambodian women. She was emphatic in her assertion that women are not subordinate to men in

Cambodian society. She gave the example of her mother, whose wishes prevailed in her family. Even her father paid heed to her advice. She also disputed the enormity of the problem of domestic violence among Cambodian women in Lowell. Her assessment was that here people have recourse to problems and can take steps to alleviate them. This was not possible in her homeland, she suggested. Upon talking to many other women and men, my confusion was clarified. While it is true that men have institutional authority, Cambodian women traditionally have a lot of leverage at home. They manage the home front. In the domestic realm, they decide and manage the affairs of the family. The everyday routine operation of the household is under women's supervision, including financially managing the home budget. In fact, it is interesting to note that many of the Cambodian grocery and jewelry shops that I have visited in Lowell are run and managed by women. In a news bulletin that I read in the Internet, it was reported that women in Cambodia are playing a leading role in propelling its economy that is unprecedented in the world.[39] So, while officially the men are invested with institutional power and women are legally subordinate to them, women are not totally subservient to men. One elderly woman that I interviewed pointed out that Cambodian women have a more difficult time here because of their dual responsibilities on two fronts: the home and outside. Working outside the home may add to their stress like women elsewhere around the world. But it may also empower them, and their husbands may not feel comfortable with their newly found autonomy.[40] Labor force participation for Cambodian women in Lowell has been liberating. A common response by women repeated to me time and again was "here in this country you can do anything you want." This was an obvious reference to freedoms experienced by women in American society, which they had also tasted and enjoyed.

This newly found freedom could underlie the problem of domestic violence in the community that has drawn enough public attention to merit a task force to address this problem. A colleague of mine who is involved with the Cambodian community in Lowell indicated to me the psychological slide that Cambodian men experience as they lose their authority in the family due to women's gainful employment. A similar phenomenon has been noted among working-class men in America who have lost their predominant role of economic providers in their families with the structural changes in the economy.[41] Women's accessibility to resources affecting men's behavior is also documented in other ethnic communities and leads to gender tensions.[42]

Domestic Abuse

The problem of domestic violence among Asians in the United States is only now being discovered due to the public consciousness of this as a social problem. Even so, women as victims do not easily share this information because of the humiliation they feel. Out of a total of twenty-five women I interviewed, only two reported having experienced or witnessed it. The first case was reported by a young woman who acknowledged seeing her stepfather abuse her mother; and the other case was an adult woman who was severely battered by her husband. In my interview with the latter, she did not mention being abused by her husband in Cambodia. She and her husband had been together weathering the troubles and hardships that escape from Cambodia entailed under Pol Pot's regime. It seems her problems may have been aggravated by her acceptance of some U.S. ways, such as the use of cosmetics to enhance her looks. She mentioned how her husband did not like her to wear any makeup and became very angry when she did. She also found him to be sexually abusive toward one of her children. Her marriage ended in divorce. She was able to divorce her abusive husband with the help of a friend whom she refers to as her mother. She had also been sponsored by this woman. As part of the divorce settlement, she lost custody of her six children. Her ex-husband, she said had "poisoned" her children against her. This caused her a lot of pain. In due time she remarried another man. They jointly bought a home in which they now live. Both she and her husband work, and she seems to be quite busy with her life, work, home, and the church that she goes to regularly. She converted from Buddhism to Christianity upon coming to the United States and seems to have found peace in her life.

Issues of Identity

Sarika talked about how Cambodians are lumped with other Asians, especially Chinese, and this bothered her. She wanted to be recognized as a Cambodian with her distinct group identity. She emphasized the importance of retaining one's identity but added that Cambodians are viewed negatively because "they are seen as being on public assistance" and as "gangsters." She noted that there was an "element of racism in American attitude toward Cambodians." She saw herself as more American than Cambodian, and this may be in reference to the fact that she is not as inhibited to speak up her mind as Cambodian girls/women are. She liked the freedom to speak and behave in accordance with her preference, although she also lamented the existence of "too much freedom" in American society.

Nary also noted that Cambodians are lumped together with other Asians and are looked down upon by Americans as "lower to them." She too viewed herself as Cambodian and added she could never consider herself as an American. She was not a U.S. citizen but would become one for job opportunities. Mak mentioned earlier sees herself as Cambodian American. She is a U.S. citizen and wants to stay here. "This is home," she said. However, she too noted the negativity with which Americans viewed the Cambodians, "living in crowded quarters" and "children in gangs."

Tida was fifty-one years old and had four children, two sons and two daughters. She identified herself as being Khmer. She lamented the fact that Khmer traditions were disappearing among the young. Only the elders in the community are maintaining the traditions. She noted that going to the temple was important for continuity of Khmer traditions, and all people have to be involved in it. An individual alone cannot do it. She was concerned about the behavior of children in schools and noted parents and teachers do not have the same kind of authority over their children as they did in Cambodia. She had heard of children hitting their teachers here. This would never happen in her homeland, she said. She also spoke of her language deficiency that prevented her from becoming a citizen of the United States.

Mea is sixty-seven years old. She noted the difficulty of assimilating into American society due to language difficulties in English. She defined herself as Khmer. She was proud of her ethnicity and spoke of the traits that Americans can learn from the Cambodians. She noted that "Americans don't like Cambodians because of bad things such as gangs." There is a lot of gang activity, which disturbs the peace of the community. She noted that others such as Puerto Ricans were also involved in such activities.

Golap was thirty-two years old when I first met her. She talked about prejudice of Americans toward Cambodians. She said Americans see "Cambodians as sloppy . . . uneducated, backward" and "with bad hygiene." She had personally been treated differentially at work and noted the differences between Americans and Cambodians in many different aspects, including friendships and relationships. She identified herself as Khmer first, although she liked the equality she experiences in her personal life. The day I went to meet her for the first time she was at work. What struck me was that her husband was feeding her child in the car while she was in the office talking to me. She was the mother of an infant, and during his lunch break he brought the baby so Golap could see her.

The perceptions of identity by how the women (cited above) see themselves and how the society at large sees the ethnic group they belong to are disparate. All these women recognize their Khmer identity and are proud of their heritage. However, they are also aware of the negativity with which their community is viewed by the larger society. What is further interesting is the sentiment expressed in a seminar I attended recently on refugee experiences of Cambodians in Lowell. Some participants spoke of their feelings of lack of belongingness in this city. Although they lived among large numbers of Cambodians, they still felt as being not part of the American society. In fact, both of the two people who voiced such feeling had come as child refugees and had grown up here. They are both successful and have professional jobs. Journeys they have made from the time they first arrived in Lowell to the present time are noteworthy. Yet when these individuals made trips to their homeland recently, they felt happy that they were among their own people. There was of sense of "being among your own" that they never felt in Lowell. In a phone conversation that I had with one of the participants, she said it is "the difference" that makes her feel that way. What she was referring to is the schism that divides the dominant group from those who are physically and culturally distinct.

The foregoing pages describe the social and human issues encountered by Cambodians in their attempts to resettle in their new homeland. As they go about the business of living and meeting their needs, attempting to raise children and maintain their cultural ways, they also encounter problems. Some of these are minor and others are serious. The process of adaptation is multifaced and complex. Migration to a new land involves daunting challenges. Some problems may be anticipated and others are unexpected. Migration entails a mixture of costs and rewards. Gains (rewards) and losses (costs) go hand in hand. Some gains entail some losses too. As the Cambodians have resettled in Lowell like other immigrants before them, they have faced personal and social challenges, some of which has been particularly difficult to adjust to. The new ways of thinking and acting that American cultural scripts require have been particularly problematic for the older generation of adults with little or no language competency skills essential to function in this country. Some older Cambodian women have been handicapped by their inability to access basic opportunities because of their lack of language skills. Other women have had opportunities open to them, opportunities for material welfare and personal fulfillment. Some have succeeded in accomplishing goals that they had set for themselves. Across the board one thing that all the women expressed is the freedom to be and to do what they want. However, this freedom also made them vulnerable to fail if they did not have the combination of skills that is essential for successful adaptation. Women trying to make a living and a life for themselves in a different cultural context, the knowledge that they are not the only ones encountering problems, can be therapeutic and empowering to them. They can be comforted in the awareness that some of these problems are not of their own making. It is part of the process of resettlement. What needs to be done is to give them the tools with which they can help themselves.

CHAPTER FIVE

From Tradition to Modern: Family Changes Among Cambodian Women

Coming to America provided the Cambodian refugees freedom from violence and terror that they sought to escape. However, they were straddled with demands that entailed new conflicts and struggles not envisioned when journeys were undertaken. The United States has provided Cambodian refugees with opportunities of life and liberty and to start anew. However, as the previous chapter illustrated, the process has not been problem free. Dynamics of family and personal relationships have been affected and altered. So have self-definitions and personal goals. While being in America is desirable, becoming "American" may not necessarily be so.[1] Like many Asians who have come before them, Cambodian refugees are also encountering the dilemma of juggling between two different social worlds: practices of their homeland and those of U.S. society and culture. This is a dilemma that has always plagued generations of immigrants and their children. For parents coming from regions of the world where sexuality is rigidly controlled, raising children is fraught with anxiety, especially when they come of age. The first generation are likely to encourage their children to subscribe to traditional gender practices while the second generation is likely to lean towards what is American and in vogue. Thus, international migration is associated with generational tension regarding sex, love, and marriage norms and values. In this chapter the family stories of the women interviewed for this study are described and issues of the sex and marriage practices these reveal are examined.

Marriage Tradition: Old Versus the New

In much of the world where marriages are arranged by parents and/or relatives, it is considered far too important an alliance to be left absolutely to the individuals. If one examines societies around the world, it is only very recently that the idea of love and sexual attraction and sexuality have become important in the selection of partners in life. This is especially true in the developed countries of the world. In United States, for instance, the rights of the individual in managing his or her own personal familial life evolved with the changing foundations of the economy from an agrarian to an industrial economy. The family formation process moved from the arena of family control to that of the individuals when dating emerged on the social scene sometime in the early part of the twentieth century. As individuals began to earn wages in their own rights, they had a greater voice in their own affairs. This was reinforced by the idea of individualism that permeated the society in general. As Western and modern ways of life have spread globally, the values of rights of the individual and individualism have gained ideological significance. Immigrants and children of immigrant living within the borders of this country have also been influenced by this ideology, as will be shown through some of the cases discussed below.

In societies where arranged marriages prevail, marriages are considered to be public and social affairs rather than personal and individual. Parents and close sets of relatives are involved in the process of mate selection of their children; they must consent to and arrange the marriages of their children. A marriage broker or a go-between brings a proposal to the families involved; if the parties agree to the match and approve of it, the process of "arranging" a marriage then shifts to the parents. The individuals to be married do not take an active role in fixing their own marriages. In Cambodia, the marriage process starts with a few steps leading to the arrangement of the marriage when these steps are completed. The process begins with the mediator meeting with the girl's parents. After a satisfactory search into the character of the girl and/or the boy by the respective parties, the parents agree to the match. The engagement ceremony is then held, which involves giving of gifts of jewelry and new clothes, as well as other gifts. The wedding ceremony is held at home, and the feast may be at home or in a restaurant. The expenses for the wedding are usually borne by the man.[2] Sometimes friends may agree to arrange marriages among their children. Marriages are also arranged among cousins. Cousin marriages are reported to occur in many parts of the world, and in some areas these are considered the most preferred potential mates.

In traditional societies, there are strict rules against mixing between sexes before marriage. Dating or heterosexual mixing as a prelude to marriage as known in the United States or the Western world is absent. As social affairs, marriages are never a matter of individual choice for a couple alone. In fact, romantic love is considered risky and frowned upon. Any display of physical intimacy before marriage is considered to be inappropriate or downright immoral. Many Cambodian women in my study have indicated this, even those who deviated from the tradition themselves. Romantic love or physical attraction is indeed considered irrelevant for good marriages. It is interesting to note that even in the United States romantic love was considered dangerous as a basis of lasting and true relationship even as late as the third quarter of the 19th century.[3] Marriages were linked to the economic and social needs of the community where issues of economic stability and security played an important role in the marital decision-making process. By contrast, today it is considered natural and normal for people to want to marry someone for love and personal fulfillment. Indeed, the idea of arranging marriages seems unacceptable and strange from the responses that I elicit from students in my classes when I tell them that I did not know the man I married, and my marriage was an arranged one.

One of the tensions children of parents who are immigrants/refugees experience growing up in America revolves round the issue of dating and hanging out with friends of the opposite sex. This is true of Cambodian adolescents just as it is true of other Asian children who are growing up and coming of age in the United States. One Asian student in my class interestingly blamed her grandmother for her not having a partner from her homeland. She alleged that her grandmother is to blame because this situation would never have arisen if her grandmother had not migrated to this country. Many Cambodian students in my classes have expressed the tussle they experience with their parents because of the confrontation of two different value systems associated with the marriage selection process and who is considered to be a desirable mate. Groups that have come to this country in the past several decades are confronted with the issue of transmission of their ethnic identity and culture to the next generation. One way of assuring the continuity of this identity and culture is to have children marry people selected for them by parents from within their communities. Men and women in Cambodia do not date as a prelude to marriage.

Cambodian marriages, as noted above, were traditionally arranged. Premarital sex was abhorred. Some traits and attributes were considered desirable in potential mates. Of course, these preferences were defined by gender and were not uniform for men and women. By and large, double standards prevailed, and qualities that made a woman good were emphasized for girls. Physical intimacy before marriage was not encouraged; opportunity for it was limited, given the nature and organization of society in Cambodia. Indeed, public display of physical intimacy by couples prior to or after marriage in Cambodia was very improbable given the public scrutiny individuals were subject to in their communities. Even husbands and wives do not show affection to each other publicly, such as kissing each other or being physically close in front of their children. The price of sexual freedom was particularly burdensome for women. Any kind of rumor involving a woman's being licentious was damaging for a family's reputation. Sexuality of an unmarried daughter was specially likened to spoilt meat that attracts flies (men).[4] A woman known to be "fooling around" or having an affair would not be considered a desirable match and would not be sought after for marriage. Even if the two people knew each other and were interested in marrying, their marriage was still arranged by their parents and thus was in conformity to the traditional process. The family was far more important than the individual.

This model of marriage is in sharp contrast to the dominant idea of marriage that exists in the U.S. where the individual chooses and decides on his or her partner and "falling in love" is considered to be important and necessary for marriage. Romantic love is glorified. The idea of romantic love is a powerful cultural ideal because it invests the responsibility of choice of mate to the individual concerned rather than the family to which the individual belongs. Children growing up in the United States are drawn to it both for cultural and structural reasons. Structurally, there are opportunities for individuals to meet, to discover and pursue this idea, whether it is at school or at work. Once out of the home, parents cannot monitor the activities of their children, especially if parents have to work for wages outside the home. The freedom of choice embedded in the idea of romantic love is culturally very attractive also. It is this that makes for tension and generational conflict between parents and children. As stated above, this is not an isolated phenomenon with the Cambodian refugees alone. In fact, there are records of other ethnic groups who have gone through this process of change and challenge as they have settled in the U.S. The Chinese, who came much earlier, defied parental choices by working arrangements of group dating where members of the opposite sex could meet in "American style" dating while not totally abandoning old world mores and thereby scandalizing their community members.[5] This was in the first quarter of the twentieth century. As recently as the latter part of the 1990s, I remember having a conversation with a white male student in my class who reported he could not visit his Portuguese girlfriend in her house in Lowell because her parents disapproved of their relationship. More recent ethnic groups from different parts of the subcontinent of India also have experienced tension in their communities between preserving and continuing the "old" marriage traditions versus adopting the "new" modern ones. I have seen parents attempting to direct their children, especially girls, to the "desirable" tracks but often succumbing to failure when their children resist strongly.

More than four decades ago, William J. Goode wrote about world revolution in family patterns referring to the changes taking place in family structures and relations around the world. Although he critiqued the simple causal relation between economic and technological factors as prime movers of family changes, his basic observation was that economic expansion via industrial systems lead to changes in family patterns, and in this movement courtship and mutual attraction gain higher value. And in this process ideological changes independent of industrial processes have an effect on family action.[6] Since then, other writers have also written about global changes taking place in family norms and relations wherein the traditional family norms are being replaced by more democratic family norms endowing individuals a greater voice in managing their own lives. The trend toward democracy and individual rights in family relations is seen in many regions of the world, including regions of the world such as China and India known for their traditional family norms. Nowhere is this change more visible than the developed countries of the world of which the United States is a prime example. Family changes in the United States are noticeable if one examines the demographic data relating to such things at cohabitation, age at marriage, rates of marriage, divorce, fertility patterns, and life course. Ethnic groups arriving in the U.S. have not been exempt from the influence of forces prevailing in this society, and this comes to a head as children come of age and have to make choices relating to starting their own families. Migration is not an easy process, even when it is intentional. Consequently, one notices that many immigrants after arrival in the U.S. find themselves in a tussle between the old and the new. For example, many immigrant families find themselves in a situation where they encounter problems trying to get their children to maintain and adhere to customary standards of behavior that they had grown up with. At the same time, they want their children to avail of the opportunities that will lead them to economic success. And here lies the dilemma. In going through the schools and educational system, the children not only learn skills and tools that will make them economically viable in this country, they also learn ways of thinking and behaving that may be at odds with the traditional norms of their parents. Education is thus a double-edged sword. While it prepares you for the new, it also challenges the old.

    A Cambodian woman in her early thirties whom I have known for some years reported that there was a lot of pressure put upon her by her parents to get married. When I asked her if she was looking for a partner, she reported that she was not really interested and also that is not the way things are traditionally done. It is the friends or relatives who bring a proposal to the girl's parents, as noted earlier, and at her age, it was difficult to find a match. In Cambodia the appropriate age of marriage for girls is in the teens, reported many women in my study. While she was pursuing her education in preparation for her career choice, she had support of her parents. However, her parents also wantd her to settle down. She seems to be not keen to do so. The fact that she has thus far been able to resist parental pressure and remain single is indicative of both the change and continuity of Khmer cultural norms. In pursuing educational and career goals that she and her parents wanted, she has gone past the "marriage age." At the same time, the pressure exerted upon her to marry indicates the desire to conform to tradition in a culture where marriage is considered to be the appropriate goal for women. Of course marriage and family processes and patterns that existed in the homeland are not exactly replicated in the resettled communities. While traditions are not altogether abandoned, some new patterns are emerging that mark a departure from traditional cultural standards.

Much diversity is noticeable in ways in which family formation is taking place among Cambodians in the U.S. Some of the older women interviewed for this study had been married traditionally by their parents when they were in Cambodia. Some among them had resisted the proposals that were put forth by their parents and were eventually married to spouses that they wanted to marry. One woman had her marriage arranged in the labor camp by the Pol Pot soldiers. A fifty-one-year-old woman who stayed at home with her husband due to health problems reported that she was married by her parents and preferred to have the tradition of Cambodian marriage continue but was not sure what her children would do. Another woman, a mother of several sons, had her marriage arranged but not to the person that her parents had initially wanted her to accept. Among the younger women interviewed who were married in this country, some had been married with parental involvement or pressure, and others had chosen their mates themselves. A woman who worked in an organization providing family services to young parents indicated that she had seen some parents arrange marriage of their teenage daughters to much older men because they were seen as successful and stable. This arrangement of marriage of a girl fifteen years old to a man who was thirty years old was out of love for their child. Since the man had a stable job, he was seen as a better son in law than a younger man who was without a job but closer in age. Many parents began to examine the credentials of a boyfriend once they discovered their daughter was dating the boy. Marriage was respectable and had the support of public opinion in their community.[7] These women exemplify the diversity in family formation and the persistence of tradition as well as change in family forms and relationships.

Migration and Change

All the women in this study were foreign born. They came as refugees after the United States agreed to take them following the world attention given to their plight due to the atrocities committed by the Khmer Rouge government under Pol Pot's rule. Some of the young women interviewed in this study had come to this country as children and had gone to schools in the U.S. Others had come here as adults with very young children who came of age in America. Adults who were already married at the point of entry in this country had their marriages arranged for them, even if they knew their spouses before marriage. The young adults in this study who came to the U.S. as children and went to schools here, however, have a more diverse record. Some of them had their marriages arranged for them, while others had charted courses of actions that were nontraditional. These include women defying their parents and marrying by self-selecting; women living with their partners prior to marriage (whom they later married); and others who left their partners even though they became pregnant and gave birth to children out of wedlock. These indeed mark significant departures from the traditional Cambodian standards of sexuality and marriage noted earlier. In a span of two decades since their arrival, Cambodians are engaging in forms of behavior characteristic of Americans in this country who have lived through a period of significant cultural and social revolution. It is these forms of family behavior that are described below.

The Cases

Savanna was twenty-seven years old when I first met her. She kept talking about having a boyfriend that she lived with, which came as a surprise to me having learned from some of my informants how physical sexual relationship before marriage between the sexes was traditionally frowned upon by Cambodians. Only later in our conversation did it become clear that she had been married in a religious ceremony by the monks, but her marriage was not considered legal, so she was told by a lawyer, since she did not get a marriage license that the State of Massachusetts required. The man she lived with whom she referred to as her boyfriend was indeed her husband whom she had married according to the Cambodian social customs. The events leading to her marriage are interesting and reflect the force of tradition.

Savanna was involved in match making for her friend: she was trying to introduce her friend to the man she ended up marrying. As she attempted to play cupid for her friend, a relative saw her with the man that she was trying to match her friend with. This was reported to her parents, who were told of this brewing romance between her and this man that she had been seen with. Rather than have her continue "this romance," she was pressured to marry him. Since she was very much under the control of her family and not allowed any freedom that she desired, she succumbed to the pressure and got married. This was also her way to get out of the house. She quit school after her marriage (she was a teenager at the time) and within a year was pregnant with her first child. When I interviewed her at age twenty-seven, she was already a mother of two young boys. She was working full time and going to classes at night trying to complete a degree in psychology. Savanna was forced to marry when she was in her teens because her parents did not want her to be involved with a man in a premarital romantic relationship that they thought was happening. She had her marriage arranged by her parents who thought it best to marry her off rather than have her courted by a man. A Buddhist monk performed her marriage ceremony, which was recognized as a legitimate union in the community. However, such unions were not considered legal in the state because the legal process of marriage was not completed. A woman who worked in the community delivering service to the Cambodians told me that such unions were problematic, especially for women if the relationship ended in separation. If the relationship failed, women so married could not claim any compensation due to the rights and privileges associated with legal marriage.

Sarika was twenty years old when I first interviewed her. She was nine years old when she came into this country. She also was in a Thai refugee camp before she came to this country with her sister and her brother-in-law. It was his relative who had sponsored them to this country. Her mother remained in Cambodia because she was too old to travel, so her older sister was her surrogate parent in this country. She lived with her older sister until she was married at the age of fourteen. Her sister had her married "the honorable way," rather than run away. This was a reference to a situation where she could have run away or eloped or end up having sex and get pregnant. She mentioned that her classmate in the seventh grade had become pregnant. Talking to her, I was left with the feeling that Sarika was married early by her guardian to avoid the situation that she saw adolescents in her community fall prey to. Marriage was respectable, Sarika noted. However, her marriage ended up in the same end result that her sister had hoped to shield her from—early pregnancy. When I met Sarika, she was a single mother with a son who was around six years old. Her marriage had ended in divorce. The source of conflict and subsequent marital dissolution came when she discovered that her husband was fooling around with other girls. There was unpleasantness at home, where she was confined to domestic duties, coupled with lack of sympathy from her in-laws who she felt interfered in her domestic conflict. She broke up with her husband when she was a junior in high school. In leaving her marriage, she found freedom both from her unfaithful husband and domestic conflict. After her breakup, she started going out with other men and was much talked about for doing so. However, the gossip did not bother her. She believed that those who criticized her were not entitled to do so because they did not give her any help in raising her child. As a senior in college, she had a boyfriend with whom she hoped she would be able to start a new chapter in her life. When I met her a few years later she had not remarried although she acknowledged having a physically intimate relationship with her former boyfriend.

Nary came to this country at the age of eleven with her widowed mother (her father had been killed by the Khmer Rouge) and two siblings, a brother and sister. She had spent several years in different refugee camps in Thailand before she came to this country. At the time I interviewed her, she was in college majoring in one of the social sciences. She spoke of some of the problems she encountered in this society due to prejudice and racism; she also spoke of the positive aspects of American society, which included the opportunities for education and the freedom she had for self-discovery and awareness, which she thought was "mind opening." Her liberal arts education in college may have predisposed her to question some of the traditional customs in her own community.

In Cambodia before the revolution young girls would quit school after primary education. Reading and writing were discouraged in women, as that knowledge was likely to give them the freedom to write "love letters."[8] Limiting the opportunity for education for girls kept them tradition bound and not deviating from accepted gender practices. Nary's example illustrates the reason why women in Cambodia were not given the opportunity for education.

Pressure was put on Nary to arrange her marriage when she was a freshman/sophomore in high school. This could very well be a preemptive attempt by her elders to prevent her from having sexual liaisons before marriage, because pregnancy outside of marriage would be undesirable and lead to loss of face in the community. Upholding family honor was important; a person's actions determined the honor of the family, and family identity took precedence over individual choices and desires. Nary reported that she had heard of eighteen-year-old Cambodian girls becoming pregnant without getting married. In fact, I had also heard of incidences of premarital teenage pregnancy among Cambodian adolescents from some of my informants. Many mothers whom I interviewed were very critical of the freedoms provided to children in this country, and they were concerned about the consequences. Thus, it is not surprising that some parents concerned about the dangers of this freedom attempted to arrange the marriages of their daughters early, as attested by the cases cited above. These arrangements were a way to thwart any such occurrence from happening in their own families. A woman associated with a church in Lowell involved in refugee rehabilitation work told me of a family where an academically very bright girl was married soon after high school graduation to prevent her from making choices that could jeopardize their family's reputation. Nary, however, did not marry according to the wishes of her mother. When asked about arranged marriage, she said she "could not do it." She was romantically involved with a person outside of her community who was of a different religious faith than her: She was a Buddhist and her boyfriend was Muslim. Her mother was opposed to this relationship, and in order to dissuade this affair, her mother decided to move out of Massachusetts to somewhere in the Midwest where she had relatives. The day before the family was scheduled to depart, Nary married the man she was in love with. She had defied her parent's wishes. She had exercised her own choice in her mate selection process, chosen a person that her mother was opposed to, and married him without parental consent. In a society where marriages are negotiated between persons who are considered appropriate and suitable matches, this was indeed a break from tradition and therefore indicative of ideological and behavioral changes. The attraction and love that Nary felt for her partner prompted her to go against her mother's wishes. She married the person of her choice. She was still in college when she married her partner, and before she graduated she had become pregnant, with her first child.

Marina also had come to this country as a refugee. She was twenty-two years old at the time of entry to this country. She also spent a lot of time in various refugee camps in Thailand before coming here. It was her uncle who had sponsored her to this country along with her mother and siblings. Like Nary, her father had been killed by Pol Pot. Unlike many of the Cambodian refugees who had come to this country, Marina came from the elite class in Cambodia. Her father was a high-ranking official in the government. So were many of her other relatives. Her father was multilingual. So was she. She went to school in Cambodia, and her first exposure to English was there. Marina spoke French and English in addition to Khmer, which was her mother tongue. Marina had finished high school in Baltimore and received a scholarship for undergraduate studies in college. She was majoring in computer science, but instead of finishing college she got a job as a word processor. She met the man she married on a trip to Boston when she visited a cousin. Her friendship blossomed into a full-blown romance. The man she married was a Cambodian. However, her mother was opposed to this relationship because of the differences in background between the two families. He was from a rural background. His family were farmers and came from modest and humble origins. He had limited education and worked as a machine operator. Marina, on the other hand, came from an educated urban family. Her family members held responsible and powerful position in Cambodia before the collapse of the government where the reins of power passed into the hands of the Khmer Rouge. Her mother was educated and was a teacher in the school for international children in Cambodia. Basically, Marina and her husband came from very different familial backgrounds, and this was the reason why her mother was opposed to this match. Rather than abide by her mother's wishes, Marina eloped with the man she was in love with and married him. A justice of peace performed the civil marriage ceremony. She moved to Lowell after her marriage. Her decision to marry against her mother's wishes created a rift in her relationship with her mother, who broke all ties with her subsequent to the marriage. It was only after the birth of her first child that the mother and daughter reconciled their relationship. But even so, Marina noted that her mother had not totally forgiven her.

Mak was twenty-eight years old when I interviewed her. She also came as a refugee with her family members that included her parents and siblings. Like the women mentioned above she too had spent some time in the refugee camps of Thailand before she arrived here in Massachusetts. It was a cousin who had sponsored her family and her. She came from a rural background in Cambodia. Her father was a farmer of moderate means and owned his own land and home. Mak has spent her adolescent years in Lowell. She has been actively involved in local community affairs and was working as a counselor in the Department of Social Services when I met her for the first time.

Mak met her partner in college where she was taking courses toward a bachelor's degree in psychology. Her partner is a white American. She had noted that her parents, like other Cambodian parents, were strict with her as she was growing up and did not allow her to go anywhere after school. In fact, even when she went to the library to study after school hours because it was noisy and crowded at home, she met with a lot of resistance and objection from her parents. She laughed and said they suspected she was "going to the library to meet boys" there. She also indicated that Cambodians did not encourage the public display of any type of physical affection between the sexes. When she had invited her boyfriend to visit her family to introduce him to her parents, they were uncomfortable seeing him sit "so close to her." Mak also noted that Cambodians do not favor living together before marriage. Yet Mak, who was engaged to her partner for two years before marrying him, moved in with him in the house they had jointly bought before getting married. When I had interviewed her subsequently, she was living with her boyfriend in the same house. Her sister's family was also living with her. She got married to her partner before the birth of her children, so her children were not born out of wedlock. In a subsequent meeting after the birth of her first child, when I had asked Mak about her parent's attitude toward her living with her partner before marriage, she noted that her parents had recognized her union with her partner as one akin to marriage. Another young woman living with her boyfriend out of wedlock also expressed similar views. When a couple cohabits, she had noted that the relationship is recognized as being one of marriage. This may be a way of conferring legitimacy to a situation that traditionally would be unacceptable.

Bopha was two years old when she came to this country as a refugee with her parents. At the time I interviewed her she was twenty years old. She is a high school graduate. Her parents have been married for forty years. They were married in Cambodia, and their marriage was an arranged one. Bopha mentioned that her parents would prefer to have her also marry via arrangement. Bopha, however, is very critical of arranged marriages. When asked about arranged marriages, she remarked "not a good idea for me." When she was fourteen years old, she started dating a Laotian boy who was a year older than her. That relationship did not last, and they ended breaking up. She conceded that she was too young then. Her parents were kept in the dark about this relationship. When she was seventeen years old, she started dating a Cambodian boy. She told her mother about him, and her mother was not very happy to learn about this relationship. Her mother did not want her to continue the relationship "unless she got married" to him. There was a lot of disagreement and conflict between the mother and daughter, and finally Bopha left the house in order to end this conflict. Her mother also wanted her out of the house because of the affair that she did not approve of.

After leaving her parental home, Bopha moved in with her boyfriend's family. She was supposed to have been engaged to him but was not. However, she was already viewed as their son's wife by his parents. She lived in that household for over a year. She became pregnant while she was living with her boyfriend. She was not happy there. It was a conflict-ridden family and her boyfriend was abusive toward her. She also reported that his mother was not very nice to her and always took her son's side. When I met Bopha, she was visibly pregnant. She had moved back with her parents, although she was expecting a baby and had not married the father of the baby. Her mother took her back because she (her mother) would "rather have her pregnant than be with an abusive man." Bopha, referring to her premarital pregnancy, mentioned that this would never have happened in Cambodia where dating is forbidden and opportunities for the sexes to be intimate unavailable. Her mother was not happy with her dating and subsequent pregnancy and yet refrained from saying "I told you so." According to Bopha, she was in a lot of pain and frustration because of the events surrounding Bopha's action. Her parents are traditional and still would prefer that she had married before becoming pregnant. However, Bopha is vehemently opposed to an arranged match. What is interesting is that Bopha's sister is also living with her boyfriend in her parent's house, although she too is not married to him.

Chanda was two years old when she came to this country as a refugee from Thailand. She came to this country with her parents and other relatives such as her grandmother. Her parents divorced after being in this country for a few years. Her mother did not remarry, although she started living with another man, a white American. Chanda noted that living together "is considered the same as marriage in the Cambodian culture."

Chanda spoke unaccented English, and if one heard her without looking at her, one would not know that she was of Cambodian heritage. She had gone through the public school system and had graduated from high school. While in school she began to feel discontent for not being allowed to do the things that girls her age are known to engage in, such as attending school dances, going to the mall and the movies. She began to have problems with her mother. Her mother felt she was becoming too "American" while she felt her mother was being unreasonable and did not understand the needs of a teenager.

It was in high school that she met a boy with whom she became very friendly. Soon their relationship developed into an intimate one. She introduced her boyfriend to her mother, who accepted him, realizing that in America this is the way things were done. After graduating from high school, Chanda got engaged to her boyfriend. It was at this time that she realized that she was also pregnant, and he was the father of her child. Rather than stay in her parental house and be dependent on them, she decided to move in with her boyfriend. With the birth of her child, she became a young mother while she was also working part time and going to school at the same time. Her boyfriend also worked to support them. Her life as a wife, mother, student, and worker became very stressful. This led to a rift in their relationship when she discovered that while she was trying to keep everything together, her fiancé had not been faithful to her. He had multiple affairs while he was living with her. This was the final straw that broke their relationship, and she decided to separate from him even though that meant she would be a single mother in charge of raising her child by herself. It was his infidelity that led her to leave the relationship because she could not accept it. Her mother did not support her in this decision. She could not understand why Chanda was leaving her fiancé. Sexual infidelity in boys/men was accepted as natural and normal. It was part of the double standard of morality alluded to above. However, Chanda, on her part, thought it impossible to carry on a one-sided relationship where both parties were not equally committed to it. Devotion and commitment to one's husband even in the face of marital infidelity by him, were important virtues that women were expected to exemplify in their lives according to Cambodian norms.[9] Chanda refused to be traditional and put up with a marital "offense."

Chanti's case is different from the examples cited above. She was faced with the situation where her son wanted to marry out of the community, to a white woman of Irish descent. There are examples of white men marrying Cambodian women in Lowell that I know of where their families have approved with or without reluctance. However, the cultural equation of a Cambodian man with a white partner is uncommon and therefore is cited here.

It was at a public meeting that I met Chanti. She was full of spirit and was very happy to learn about my study and wanted to participate in it. At her invitation I went to meet her at her house where she told me about her life after she came to this country. She was married and had three sons. During the revolution she was separated from her husband. It was after many years that he joined her in the United States. There was some tension in their relationship when her husband came back because she had male friends with whom she went out. Her husband was not pleased with this development. Chanti had struggled initially to raise her sons. She worked two jobs to earn an income that would enable her to take care of her family. Her older son married a Cambodian woman whom he chose himself and she approved of. Her second son had an Irish girlfriend. He met her in high school. Chanti was very apprehensive when her son told her about it. Her main concern was whether such a relationship would endure. Chanti was not opposed to the relationship per se. In fact, she added that she didn't mind her sons marrying women of any color, white, black, or yellow. Her concern was about the welfare of the children, her grandchildren. She invited her son's girlfriend to her house and asked her if she truly loved her son. When this young Irish woman told her how much she loved her son and sought her permission to marry him, she was completely won over. Chanti asked me if I had ever heard a mother-in law being asked for such permission from a prospective bride. She recognized that this society was different and things were done differently here. She even stated that parents who arrange marriages for their children are concerned more about themselves, rather than the welfare of their children. Since this was a country with a "different civilization," it was only appropriate to understand the practices of this society and accommodate them. She cited her mother's efforts at matchmaking to her cousin, whom she did not like. Her husband was a Cambodian who had lived in Vietnam and therefore was not considered to be an appropriate match for her. She had married him despite her mother's disapproval.

Chanti was unusual. She wanted her children to have the freedom that she had experienced. She was disheartened to see the women of her country spend large amounts of money for such things as gold and jewelry, rather than engage in work to support other fellow compatriots who needed a helping hand. She regularly sent money to Cambodia to help relatives who had stayed behind. Chanti was educated; she taught French in the Thailand refugee camp where she had spend time before coming to this country. She was one of the few women who planned to go back to Cambodia to start her own business with her husband. Her case is cited here to indicate her willingness to go beyond the boundaries of her own culture and accept the choices her children made even though these mark a departure from the way things were done in Cambodia. Whether she would have acted the same if she had a daughter is a question that cannot be answered.

Thus far most of the cases cited that have been about women who were pressured to marry to thwart the possibility of romance that would embarrass their family or women who exercised their own choice and selected partners they wanted. Some of these relationships worked, and these women started their lives with their partners. Others were not so successful, and although they had children with their partners, their relationships ended in separation.

Conclusion and Analysis

These personal stories shed important light on family changes taking place among the recent Cambodian émigré to Lowell. One of the responses that I encountered almost unequivocally was the idea of personal freedom in the United States that was very appealing to the women. Coming from a very hierarchical society, this response is understandable and not surprising. However, what is interesting is that while the idea of personal freedom is attractive, it is also seen as problematic by parents. Parental control over children as they come of age is subverted. We see in the cases cited above that some of the women had exercised their own choice in selecting their life partners. In so doing, they rejected or openly opposed their parents' dictates, despite that fact that marriage and sexual matters are not entirely a matter of individual choice in Khmer society. In their adolescence, these women were governed by very strict and rigid norms of their parents, the norms their parents had experienced while growing up in Cambodia. Yet as young adults they couldn't do what their parents had done when it came to selecting their mates. All these women had entered the country as refugees and had gone through the public school system in the United States. The ages at which they entered this country varied. They grew up among their own community of people by virtue of their refugee status that entitled them to some form of governmental assistance. The irony here is that the first generation of newly emigrated groups is concerned about continuing its cultural practices such that they are replicated these in the next generation. However, the marriage and sexual norms in this country that advocates the rights of the individual are an anathema for cultural continuity of marriage and family traditions imported from homeland. Parents are especially anxious about too much freedom given to children in this country, and in the context of their traditional marriage arrangements one can recognize the reason for this anxiety. In a culture where women's sexuality is seen as dangerous because women are seen as unable to "control themselves when they are in love"[10] the availability of freedom of choice is viewed with suspicion. Yet parents are unable to insulate their children from dominant cultural forces of this society. In contemporary United States there are important changes happening in our personal lives regarding sexuality, marriage, and family. There are changes taking place about how we connect and form ties with others. This has been a subject of debate in the sociology of family studies where the protagonists of change view these changes as a trend toward democratization in family while the opponents view it as decline in family norms. We needn't get into the issue of ethics and morality of change, but we should attempt to understand the conditions that are fostering these changes in society and their implication for paths to family formation.

As stated more than forty years ago, William Goode had written about the global changes taking place in family patterns around the world due to the forces of industrialization and urbanization in his classic survey of societies around the world entitled *World Revolutions and Family Patterns*.[11] In it he had noted that regardless of the form of family prevalent in a society, family systems were moving toward a type that is more egalitarian in nature. These family changes were due to ideological or *value changes* taking place in society. Its significance is even more now given the acceptance of "democracy of emotions in everyday life"[12] in families. Even in traditional societies with rigid and hierarchical norms in sexual relations between men and women, there are open debates about sexuality and sexual equality. One need only look at the magazines in some of these societies that deal with contemporary social issues. Attitudes and behaviors regarding sexuality have undergone changes in the U.S. since the 1960s with the feminist movement, as well as cultural and social changes. These, coupled with technological breakthroughs, have given women greater freedom in controlling their reproductive lives. The notion of intimacy has gained priority in relationships, and the new basis of family is the dyad, the couple emotionally drawn together irrespective of whether they are married.

Children of recent immigrant groups to the U.S. who came at very young ages are particularly prone to accept the models that their peers subscribe to. As noted elsewhere, they "are more susceptible to pressures that are at odds with influences from the home."[13] Many of my young Cambodian students accept the idea of romantic love as important as a basis for emotional intimacy. Bopha, for instance, was very clear in her rejection of the traditional method of arranged marriage. Nary "broke the rules" when she dated and ultimately married the man she was romantically involved with. One Cambodian student of mine who used to come to see me quite often after class for her projects even felt comfortable to show me a her photo taken with her boyfriend showing them as a couple. This is interesting in view of the fact that traditionally any kind of physical association before marriage is frowned upon lest it give a bad reputation to the woman if the news gets around. If a woman has a boyfriend and the word gets around, then "no one will talk to her" or "look at her" and begin to avoid her.[14] Yet less than one in five marriages are arranged completely by Cambodian parents in eastern Massachusetts.[15]

As children start school they are exposed to social norms that may be at variance with those at home. Schools and places of work offer individuals an opportunity to meet and explore relationships, and this is supported by the larger code of values in society. As one person who works in an advisory position in the Lowell public school system noted, Cambodian children growing up here have not really seen Khmer culture and therefore are unlikely to accept it. Culturally, young adults find the idea of personal freedom attractive. Even those who are in favor of maintaining family traditions and customs of their native land do not completely want to live by traditional family and gender relations. Native-born children, as well as those who are foreign born, accept and embrace the idea of liberty and rights of the individual. One of the consistently voiced opinions by all the women interviewed for this study when asked what they liked about the U.S. was the opportunity to do and be what one wants. Migration thus is associated with revolutionary changes in values. Even though the parent generation is anxious about and inclined towards perpetuating the traditional marriage and sex practices, the second generation is pro-change. The values of the new generation include norms and ways of behaving congruent with rights of personal freedom and individual choice that they see among their peers and classmates in schools as well as outside it. When the traditional system of sex and marriage norms are juxtaposed with the new ones, often it is the latter that one chooses. This is seen even in such departures from tradition as cohabitation. It was Mak who had indicated that when she was living together, it was accepted by her parents, traditional as they were, because in their minds they had accepted that their daughter was married. This propensity for change may be due to the lack of the first generation's ability to enforce strict traditions due to structural and cultural limitations making it difficult to control children once they are out of the home. Ultimately, however, new patterns of social relationship are emerging as Cambodians try to act according to homeland cultural standards but must accept and accommodate to living in a new environment in the U.S. As noted in a different context, Cambodians have their interpretive framework of making sense of the world around them; however, they are "rearranging and reinventing" these frameworks to make sense of immediate events.[16] This is certainly true in case of mate selection methods that are different from traditional cultural standards as practiced in their homeland.

CHAPTER SIX

Toward Empowerment: Community Institution Building

Social and cultural change is normal and constant in human life. Even in seemingly homogenous societies, if one compares two points in time separated by long periods, one is likely to see the difference between the two time periods, although one may not be aware of the changes taking place when they are happening. However, when change is rapid and dramatic, it is more visible. It invites attention and may require social intervention if the individuals affected by it so need it. Individuals, like societies, change in response to internal and external forces that act upon them. Change was foisted upon Cambodian refugees due to circumstances over which they had no control. They experienced social upheaval in their lives due to political events in their home country. Their refugee status attests to that.

Coming to the U.S., although liberating for the refugees, did not automatically ensure freedom from problems of cross-cultural adaptation that migration to a new and different land might entail. There were challenges the refugees confronted. These included challenges of survival: economic, cultural, and social. As indicated in the previous chapters, there were different kinds of adjustments that had to be made as these refugees were transported into a Western cultural matrix without any or very little preparation. There were issues of language, education, conflict, or tension due to dissimilarity of culture and tradition, as well as issues of parenting children growing up in America and monitoring the process of love and marriage especially for girls. Complications of these problems were multifaceted. First, many refugees were plagued by the traumas of the war, and even though they had traveled thousands of miles to safety, there were vestiges that had lingered on. Second, many refugees had structural limitations traceable to social disadvantages associated with skill deficits necessary for survival and making it in America. Third, Cambodian émigrés as a group have a higher percentage of female-headed households with minor children. Their lives revolved around home and work, sometimes working second and third shifts, which kept them away from home and their children. This, coupled with lack of English language competency, contributed to personal and social difficulties in helping children cope with the demands of growing up in a different cultural milieu than what they had experienced growing up in Cambodia. As the refugees resettled in their new habitat, their problems surfaced. These had to be tackled for their benefit and the peace and stability of the larger community. Community activists and influential citizens in positions to help began to explore ways and means of addressing the needs of those requiring assistance. This chapter looks at some of the organizations and institutions that have been involved in empowering Cambodian refugees to a life of self-sufficiency and dignity in their new adopted homeland.

CMAA, an Ethnic Organization

As the refugees settled in Lowell, the city became the second largest ethnic enclave in the nation. This may have been a source of solace to those who needed the protection of a known and familiar ethnic environment. However, it did not necessarily lead to integration into the larger cultural matrix of mainstream society. The socially disadvantaged segment of the Cambodian community needed protection and assistance to access facilities and opportunities that would enable them a safe and viable way of life. It was for this purpose the Cambodian Mutual Assistance Association (CMAA) of Lowell was founded in 1984. This is an ethnic organization formed by and for the Cambodians to empower them to cross culturally adapt in the U.S., to improve their quality of life, and to help them realize their economic and social potential while at the same time help them retain their ethnic identity. As newcomers, Cambodian refugees were faced with many challenges that require substantial changes in lifestyles. The goal of CMAA as a grassroots ethnic organization is to serve as a conduit for the Cambodian refugee newcomers, providing them with a bridge to connect with the rest of the society. This connection is critical for the new residents' ability to traverse from the old culture that they had known in their home country to the new one into which they had settled.

Massachusetts had a refugee-friendly policy, and a lot of federal and state assistance had been funneled into Lowell to resettle the refugees. For example, Michael Dukakis, the governor of Massachusetts, in 1985 had signed an Executive Order (No. 257) that outlined his refugee policy, committing his administration to provide all state services to the refugees across the state.[1] He wrote a memo to all the state agencies instructing them to develop a policy for the future describing how they intend to serve refugees. As a consequence, many state agencies revised their eligibility forms to ensure refugee access to their services. His wife, Kitty Dukakis, took personal interest in the rehabilitation of Cambodian refugees. The *Boston Globe* reported her efforts to help refugee families reunite and settle in Massachusetts.[2] She had traveled to the refugee camps in Thailand and upon return made it a mission to help those who were the victims of the war in that area to settle here. The pro-refugee stance of the first family of Massachusetts received stinging criticism from some quarters to the point that it was even suggested by her critics, "Why she didn't take them home." Despite the official help meted out to the refugees, there were still problems encountered by the Cambodians. Those with English language competency and employable skills were able to achieve economic self-sufficiency. But others without these skills were marginalized. They needed language skill training, job training, and other forms of social support that would keep them and their families in safety and free of trouble. Social intervention to address these problems was thus essential. The CMAA was formed to deliver this much-needed assistance to new arrivals with English classes at the International Institute. It also worked with the Lowell School Department to get Khmer (native language) instruction for Cambodian schoolchildren. Most importantly, it attempted to "build confidence and a sense of self-worth." This was the first step for empowerment. Vuth Hul, a community leader in Lowell, and his brother were among those "helping to develop Cambodian self-help power and community consciousness." He emphasized the importance of being known as Cambodian in lieu of the commonly used label of "Indochinese," which was a colonial term used by the French colonizers to label groups of people from the region of Southeast Asia.[3]

The federal Office of Refugee Resettlement (ORR) provided a whole set of initiatives that led to the formation of Mutual Assistance Association (MAA) for refugee communities in the state of Massachusetts. Some leaders who were involved with community development work felt that a team of leaders within each refugee community was needed who could serve the needs of the community, since they were in a position to know them better than anyone else.[4] These teams of leaders were required to undergo training such that they could identify the needs of the community and help in addressing them. Some leaders strongly advocated that the refugees be given some basic minimum skills so that they could be self-sufficient and not have to depend upon public assistance. There was also the drive to encourage refugees to be involved and participate in the community in which they resided. Massachusetts was one of the first states in the nation to begin to push for naturalization and citizenship for refugees. It was believed that this would lead to a sense of belonging to the community and encourage the knowledge and process of community building. This happened in 1986.[5]

The CMAA in Lowell was founded in 1984 and gained funding in 1985, receiving $814,000 from the state government.[6] There were a variety of programs initiated to aid the community. These included programs for youth services, job placement programs, English as a Second Language (ESL) programs, and programs for elderly services. Although these programs were initiated through government funding and assistance, the recipients did not entirely decide what needed attention. The Office of Refugee Resettlement was in the driver's seat. It wanted to groom the people in the ethnic communities to be the service providers. This created a sense of resentment, as noted by a community activist who was in the leadership position in ORR.[7] The sense of resentment was also evident in a conversation that I had with the Executive Director of CMAA in 1995. He stated that "the government was not responsive to the needs of the community." Rather, it defined the needs from above instead of them being generated from below. The bilingual program was particularly cited as a case of an ill-conceived program where the needs of the children were ignored or indeed shortchanged. It was a transitional program, but not enough time was put into it. It was marred by a lack of uniformity, a lack of training, and a lack of adequate pay. Reasmei, one of the women who had attended the program as a child, recalled not being happy with the way the program was administered. She complained that Khmer-speaking children were isolated from other children, a fact that was unlikely to help bilingual transition.

In the early phases of its development, the CMAA was concerned with providing assistance to the refugees to address their survival needs such as housing, jobs, language classes for those without basic English language skills, transportation, and translating basic information received from government agencies. With the passage of time, more ambitious goals were incorporated. This included cultural education of children wanting to be "American" but unfamiliar with the greatness of Cambodian cultural heritage. These children were feeling the conflict of being raised by parents who wanted to be Cambodian and were untutored in "American ways." The goal of this cultural education was to tease out the difficulties involved in the parent-child relationships of family members separated by a generation as well as cultural distance. This would also promote self-esteem and prevent the children from participating in the antisocial activities that many parents feared their children would be drawn into. As noted earlier in Chapter 4, all parents that I spoke with were fearful of the influences and distractions that were out there in this society that attracted children. In order to protect their children from these influences, they resorted to strict control and discipline that only drove a further wedge between them. In a recent interview with a woman involved in helping adolescents stay away from gangs and streets, I was told that many parents forced their daughters to marry early and opposed their higher education. Some of my cases, such as Sarika and Savanna, confirm this. Indeed this woman also reported how her sister left her parent's home because of dispute over her social life. Her parents did not like her lifestyle and thought of it as bad.

There are examples of some women leaders who worked through the CMAA to bridge the gulf between parents and children, helping parents and children to respect one another and be open to each other's point of view. One such leader, Sithra Chan, who attempted to bring parents and children together, stated, "I am a bridge between the parents and the kids." Chan's goal was to help teenagers understand that growing up in America is not an either (Cambodian) or (American) proposition.[8] The CMAA Youth Corps members took it upon themselves to reach out to younger kids in middle school and listen to them and their concerns. In so doing, they were able to able to reach some Cambodian youths and deflect them from the life of the streets.

CMAA officials recognize the importance of doing well in school.[9] To help in this, CMAA provided homework assistance to kids after school. Education is the key to breaking the cycle of hopelessness that afflicts many adults and children alike. Many parents themselves were not educated; they nevertheless understood the importance of education for the welfare and future of their children. However, these parents, devoid of the appropriate know-how or the perspective on education, could not help their children with their school learning or homework. Further, their attitude toward education was different than what is accepted and expected here. A woman who spoke about her own experiences growing up in Lowell indicated the different attitudes toward education held by her parents were typical of Cambodian parents. She loved to paint and draw but did so only at night in the privacy of her bed and hid her paintings. Her parents did not see pursuit of the arts as important educational activity.

Cambodians parents were not involved in their children's education because they thought it to be the responsibility of the teachers in schools. Further, their limited communication skills prevented them from interfacing with the authorities of the schools. A Cambodian woman who worked as a liaison between parents and the school system noted how phone calls made to the family would go unanswered because the people for whom the messages were left did not respond due to their language inadequacies. They did not understand the messages.

In providing assistance with homework, the CMAA is not only attempting to achieve an educational goal but is also helping to keep kids away from harm's way. A young woman activist that I spoke with [10] noted the severe consequence among children of losing hope. It is known that the dropout rate of children unsuccessful at school is very high. After the heavy inflow of refugees in Lowell, the *Lowell Sun* reported that the official Asian dropout rate of high school students (dominated by Cambodians) was 10 percent. However, social workers in the community thought the actual numbers were higher than the official figures.[11] According to the 2000 Census data, 36.3 percent of Cambodian women in Lowell between the ages of 18 and 24 have not graduated from high school. Comparable rates for men are 38 percent. More recently, in investigating dropout rates for Cambodians, it was suggested[12] that National Center for Education figures may be a better gauge than the Department of Education dropout reports in Massachusetts. The picture that emerges is that more Cambodian children are encountering problems that lead to failures in schools. Reasons may inhere in family outlook and perspective, as well as systemic conditions embedded in the larger society of which the schools themselves are a part. Some of these children lack parental support at home. A large number of refugee women, as noted earlier, have come from very rural backgrounds and do not have any formal schooling. Many are also illiterate. Further, many Cambodian parents are reported to disapprove of American system of coeducation because boys and girls are not kept separate.[13] This is also corroborated by the woman with a college degree involved with community development work that I have spoken with who is attempting to keep children away from gangs and street violence.[14] The lack of personal and academic support for problem-ridden children and the absence of Cambodian teachers as appropriate role models have also been listed as some of the reasons for poor academic performance of Cambodian students.[15] Some CMAA leaders have taken it upon themselves to speak to parents, children, and other members of the community, emphasizing the importance of exposing children to the rich heritage of Cambodian culture and through that build hope and confidence among them.[16]

One such initiative of the CMAA that aimed to bring hope and improve the quality of life among Cambodian youth from disadvantaged backgrounds is the Light of Cambodia. It is a program where children participate in variety of activities such as art, culture, sport, and community volunteer work, all of which is geared to open their eyes and make them feel good about themselves and learn to be productive with their own lives. The goal of this initiative is to make young people self-sufficient so that they can break away from the feeling of dependence and hopelessness that condemns them to life of antisocial activities associated with a depressing social life. Another program, Future Star Sports and Leadership Development Camp, taught children lessons to keep them safe and away from the life of gangs and jails.[17] It was conceived in 1998 to keep children between the ages of 6 and 14 in summer day camps involved in sports and athletics. The program is for children at risk who have grown in neighborhoods "where gang violence ripples in persistent waves" into families with parents who survived the "killing fields" of Cambodia and are haunted by its traumas. The *Boston Globe* report on this program was positive. The newspaper reported that the children are indeed listening to the lessons because these are woven into games they play at the camp such as basketball, volleyball, and dodgeball. Although it may be difficult to gauge the effectiveness of such a program, the signs from the participants of the program seem to suggest that these work. One thirteen-year-old is reported to have said, "I never usually pay attention in class but I pay attention here," further adding "when I come here, it's safe." Sophath Pheang, who is twenty-one years old and a former gang member, joined the program as a counselor after two of his friends were killed in gang-related deaths. He joined Future Stars to break away from the street life and to help younger children stay safe and free from trouble. "Kids need a place to get off the street and I thought this was the best thing."[18] The immediate goal of the program is to help children stay safe from street violence. But the long-term goal is to help the participants to cooperate with others and develop a sense of responsibility. This program, although first conceived under the rubric of the CMAA by Sayon Soeun to stem the tide of gang violence, is now independent of it and runs as a separate organization.

It is now twenty years since CMAA came into being. It has gone through a life cycle of infancy and maturity, experiencing both good and hard times. In an interview with the present Executive Director of CMAA, whom I met recently to get some insights into the role of CMAA in helping refugees resettle, I was told that because money is tight now, the organization is hurting and unable to deliver the services needed.[19] Gang problems still exist in the community. So does poverty. In the 1990s, when the economy was doing well, there was a lot of financial support available for programs for the youth, family strength, job training, and the placement of trainees in companies. One noteworthy example that Ros personally benefited from when he was in his teens was Coalition for a Better Acre. This was a program teaching problem-solving skills to young adolescents in the community. The venue for the action was 41 Rockford Street in Lowell. This was an abandoned warehouse located to house a youth center for Cambodian teenagers. Ros and his cohort of friends had negotiated an agreement with the owner of the building, but before it could be carried through, the bank took over the building in a foreclosure. Under FDIC regulations foreclosed property had to be liquidated at 80% of the assessed value of the property. This group of kids, of which Ros was a part, had no money. They engaged in a writing campaign with the help of the principal of Bartlett School to reach the high-ranking officials whom they needed to contact. Eventually, a high-ranking official from the bank, John Pace, responded to their letters invited them to a conference meeting. The meeting was productive, and they were offered a price to buy the building. The message of this story that Ros was trying to convey was that if children are trusted with challenging tasks that give them responsibility, they are likely to take the challenges and deliver results. He was advocating this model as a way to deal with the hopelessness that afflicts many young and adult members of the community, making them vulnerable to antisocial activity such as gangs and drugs.

In the height of its success in the 1990s, the CMAA had grown to have a budget of $3.5 million to engage in many community development efforts. They were able to also negotiate ownership of a large building of their own. In a much-publicized event, the CMAA moved to a vacant building in the city's downtown area with a huge office space of which the "Cambodian Community can always be proud." However, since that acquisition, the CMAA has had problems, some of which are internal to the organization and others over which they have had no control. One issue that has affected the operation of the organization, according to a former Director, is the factionalism and disagreements about how to achieve goals of self-sufficiency for the community. In addition, the downturn in the economy has affected its ability to continue with many of its programs, such that at the present time it is engaging in self-assessment and redirecting its goals and policies so that it can continue to be a viable organization. Ros, its current Executive Director has experience in the business world and is using as business model to revive the organization into a viable outfit.

There are other ethnic organizations also in place to help with community development goals of Cambodians in Lowell. The Cambodian American League of Lowell, Inc. (CALL) was established in July 1993 to promote home ownership and spur ethnic businesses among Cambodians in Lowell. Its stated goals are to help in the economic development of the community by providing support and training in business enterprises and home ownership for people in the community. To achieve its goals, it has entered into partnership with some of the local banks and foundations.[20] As many as 100 businesses are owned by Southeast Asians in Lowell, such as jewelry and video shops, grocery stores, restaurants, and convenient stores. Some of these are managed and run by women. Two of the women I interviewed in my study now own and run their own businesses—and successfully, too. One need only look at some of the areas in Lowell to see the business centers that have sprouted up in the community in this short span of time. Families and friends have helped finance many of these business ventures, and these also employ members of the community. Through these business enterprises the community is also generating income for itself and pumping it back into the community. In the ten-year period from the mid 1990s to the present times many changes have taken place that show signs of vitality and progress. However, the report card is mixed. There are those who are still struggling. To help those who are marginalized and isolated due to language inadequacies or poverty, Southeast Asian Bilingual Advocates, Inc. (SABAI) was established. It is a nonprofit organization formed by Cambodian women in 1997. Its goal is to help women address and overcome problems of health, education, and language such that they can move on to an improved quality of life and self-sufficiency.

Religious Institutions: Churches and the Buddhist Temple

The role of religion in fostering group identity and social empowerment is documented in many sociological studies. The presence of religious networks and organizations has provided a critical forum to its leaders for advocating and planning courses of action for social improvement of disadvantaged groups. Religious leaders have often depended on church pulpits to mobilize and energize their rank and file.[21] Religion thus has served as a tool of mobilization in pursuit of social and political goals. A famous example from our recent social history comes from the Black churches in the south that were used to galvanize masses of ordinary citizens into social action against the Jim Crow laws that governed their lives. The churches provided the platform from which Black clergy and community leaders conveyed their messages to Black men and women who constituted the foot soldiers to combat the indignities that prevailed in the caste-like society of the South.

The role of the Christian church in fostering change and community empowerment has received serious scholastic attention in social science literature. Sociologists and anthropologists have written generally about the role of religion in human life. Examination of the ethnic history of the first immigrant community in Lowell reveals that when the Irish were the newcomers to town some 160 or more years ago, they had established the St. Patrick Church in 1831. It became the focal point to serve the needs of the Irish community and provide "moral, social and political guidance" to all its members.[22] Father Peter Connolly, a Catholic priest, was especially instrumental in reaching an agreement with the school committee wherein Irish immigrant children would have access to public education while the Catholics still retained some level of control over the education of their children. By reaching an agreement with the school committee and its leadership, the Catholic Church became the catalyst for social change at a time when anti-immigrant sentiment against the Irish was very much in the air. This was an example of the clergy contributing to the peace and order in the community.[23] The issue then was how to help the new immigrants coexist with the dominant Protestant groups in town without each being threatened by the presence of the other.

Almost a century and a half later the same kind of question surfaces. Only this time the ethnic groups and the religious denominations are different. The Cambodians are the newcomers in town and a large percentage of them subscribe to Buddhism, a religion that is very different from the Judeo-Christian religious traditions that have prevailed in the U.S. In the following pages we examine the role of Buddhism in aiding its members to resettle and integrate into the larger mainstream of U.S. society. In what ways is the organization of the temple harnessed to serve its people and contribute to the needs of its membership?

The first Buddhist temple in Lowell was started in 1980 in an ordinary apartment to meet and service the religious, spiritual, and cultural needs of its members. This was before the founding of the CMAA. Subsequently other temples were also established. There are two Cambodian Buddhist Temples in Lowell, both established in the 1980s. The presence of these temples, together with other factors such as availability of jobs and a burgeoning ethnic enclave, attracted a lot of secondary migrants to Lowell twenty years ago. Historically, Buddhism flourished in Southeast Asian countries such as Cambodia, Laos, and

Thailand and can be considered the state religion of these countries. Cambodia is dominantly a Buddhist country and this is reflected in the Cambodian population in Lowell. A majority of Cambodian refugees in Lowell are Buddhist (90 percent, according to one estimate). Some refugees converted to Christianity in the refugee camps prior to their arrival in the U.S. Others converted after their arrival to this country. Despite the conversion, Buddhism continues to be the dominant religion among Cambodians in Lowell. A woman I interviewed for this research had converted to Christianity because she felt she had to for all the help she had received from the missionaries in the refugee camp. Yet she also continues to believe in Buddhism and has a small shrine in her home that includes an idol of the Buddha where she offers some fruits and burns an incense stick. Her husband is a Buddhist. Most of the women I spoke to for this project were Buddhists and went to the temple for various occasions, whether to celebrate the New Year, to pray and make offerings to the monks, or observe rites following the death of a person. The temple priest is the official in charge conducting these ceremonies according to Buddhist tradition.

As a religion, Buddhism is atheistic—the idea of God is absent in it. The founder of Buddhism was an Indian prince by the name of Siddhartha Gautama born in 563 BC in northern India. The Buddha, meaning "the Enlightened One," was a title conferred on him. Siddhartha was raised in the lap of luxury; yet at the age of twenty-nine he renounced the world to seek truth and enlightenment. After six years of meditation and penance he achieved enlightenment and started teaching his disciples how to attain the Truth that he had experienced himself. He spoke of the four noble truths. The first is the idea that human existence is full of suffering. Second, the root of this suffering is human desire. Third, freedom from suffering is attainable. This is known as Nirvana and entails freedom from the cycle of birth, death, and rebirth. The fourth noble truth is that the means to achieve this is through the eight-fold path.

The school of Buddhism prevalent in Cambodia and other Southeast Asian countries is known as Thervada Buddhism. Thervada literally means "the school of the elders" and claims to perpetuate the true teachings and practices of the Buddha. It is historically older to Mahayana (Greater Vehicle), the other branch, which is the dominant tradition in the rest of the world.

Sangha (community) is the core institution of Buddhism. In Thervada Buddhism *sangha* refers to the order of monks who are responsible for dissemination of Buddha's teaching to the layman. In Cambodia, for instance, adolescents or young boys are placed in monasteries as novice monks where they learn about *dharma* (duty), *dana* (giving), *sila* (discipline), and *bhavana* (meditation).[24] The senior monks in the temple are responsible for the moral and spiritual development of the young inmates left in their charge and teach them the essential principles of Buddhism. In the temple the young boys are subject to a strong routine of learning and discipline where they learn the moral code of appropriate thought and action. Buddhism emphasizes the spiritual growth and development of the mind as means to escape the worldly cravings that are believed to be the cause of suffering in life. However, Buddhism also emphasizes service and responsibility to family, friends and the community at large as important goals of human action. The Buddha was "the world's greatest and first social worker."[25] Individuals acting selflessly in the service of the community were considered to be earning merit that contributed to their freedom from the cycle of suffering. The performance of one's duty thus connected the individual with the welfare of the community at large. The monks in their capacity as teachers of Buddhist precepts to their pupils have a religious and a secular role crucial for the maintenance of a civil society. The temple thus offers the community a physical space as well as a social one. It is through its auspices that untutored individuals can become socially responsible members of the community.

Cambodian refugees in the U.S. have build temples in an effort to restore and retain their culture and tradition as a people. Peter Rose, in a documentary produced about the Cambodian refugees, has observed that the religion of Buddhism has served as a significant tool of cultural transition for Cambodian refugees in America who have survived death and destruction in their homeland.[26] At the same time, in the same documentary, both Buddhist monks and lay followers spread in different communities across the U.S. noted the difficulties of being a Cambodian Buddhist in the United States due to the differences in the culture and values of the two societies. The monks have to wear the monk's attire and walk barefoot. They beg for alms in the morning and in the evening are the educators of Buddha's teachings in the temples. This austere routine is not possible in the U.S., physically or socially. The temples in Lowell, although the venue for hosting many individual and communal ceremonies, does not operate as an educational institution in ways that temples functioned in the homeland.[27] Even so there have been as many as eighty temples built nationwide in the United States since the Cambodians arrived as refugees to this country.

The Triratanaram Temple, one of the two Cambodian temples in Lowell, was founded in 1985 by Venerable Sao Khon under the sponsorship of Venerable Maha Ghosananda of Providence, Rhode Island. The presence of the temple was important for community building. It acted as a magnet, drawing many secondary migrants into the community. The temple provides a meeting ground for people, thus facilitating network formation within the community.[28] More importantly, the senior monk of this temple has engaged in a partnership with another government agency, namely the police department, to combat the growing tide of teen gang violence in the city among Cambodian youths. The police department, having failed in previous outreach projects to curtail gang-related crimes, has turned to religion to prevent gang members from committing serious crimes.[29] The attempt to recruit monks to help the city with the youth-related problems in the Southeast Asian community got a boost with the addition of Chanda Soth as project assistant to the Weed and Seed program in March 2003.[30] She has been active in the temple and had a close connection to the monk Venerable Sao Khon of the temple, also the president of the Buddhist Monks in the U.S. The program targets runaway troubled youths in an effort to prevent them from engaging in gang-related criminal behavior. The monks teach troubled runaway kids how to be good students and exemplary Buddhists. They spend two nights a week at the temple, more if they want. There they learn from the monks how to improve themselves "inside out and become better citizens, students, and Buddhists." Venerable Sao Khon believes this program is unprecedented among Buddhists in the United States, and he has received inquiries about this program from police departments and temples around the country.[31] The use of the temple to help troubled kids to be free of trouble is reminiscent of the monks' role in Cambodia to help community and family members resolve and cope with the problems confronting them. Commenting on the temple's involvement in this program, Soth has stated that he (Khon) "is happy that Buddhism will change the kids from bad to good."[32] The program starts with an assessment of each youth's knowledge of Buddhism and skills at meditation. From there on the lessons are personalized to meet individual needs. Captain DeMoura of the Lowell Police Department believes that the program is likely to work because of the high esteem in which the religious leaders are held in the Southeast Asian community. "The kids really believe in their religious leaders . . . more so than Catholics or others," he is quoted in the *Lowell Sun* article mentioned above. Enlisting the help of religious leaders who are revered by the community seems to be prudent way of using existing community resources and gives credence to the idea that the temple is a public space for bringing the individual and the community together.

This program was short-lived and has not continued after its initial phase. However, some community leaders that I have spoken with have suggested that city officials/authorities really do not understand Buddhism and have not invested the human resources needed to control this problem. The temple subsists on donations from its clients, many of whom are of moderate means and do not have the resources to fight this problem on their own. Further, they contend the issue is related to poverty and lack of opportunities that lead to the cycle of despair and hopelessness that leads children to the street and the life associated with it. Unless that is addressed, the problems of the youth are unlikely to be solved. More recently, the temple has been marred by conflicts of its own with the temple being divided in upstairs and downstairs factions and the two groups are not on speaking terms. With such a situation can the temple leaders hope to serve their clients in peace-making efforts, asked one community leader? What kind of example does this present to the young ones? he asked.[33] The division within the temple is demoralizing, said another woman who participated in this study. She said she had stopped going to the temple and worships at home. Interestingly, another person noted that respecting monks might be a problem for the youths as their level of knowledge is lower than the youths that are better educated.[34]

Some Cambodians have also adopted the faith of the church that sponsored them from the refugee camps of Thailand. One woman explained this by saying that the Christian churches had outreach programs that served as an incentive to convert. Another suggested that in Buddhism one could never escape from the fruits of one's deeds. But in Christianity that is not so. She converted to Christianity in obligation to the help that she received in coming to this country. Her husband did not convert. As stated elsewhere, to be a Khmer is to be a Buddhist and despite conversion to a new faith, the Buddhist values in their lives are not lost. Some women in my study were critical of those who had converted to Christianity. This is also documented by Smith-Hefner: Individuals who convert are accused for "having forgotten their culture."[35]

Cultural Events and Organizations

As people travel from one area to another and settle down in new locations forming new communities, they also import cultural items and ideas with them. In a famous article written by Ralph Linton almost six decades ago, he cited several items of culture that we think of being 100% American that are borrowed from different parts of the world, from the Middle East to the Far East. In the last thirty or more years that I have been in this country, I have seen some of the visible changes not only in Lowell but American society in general from food and cuisine to art and ways of keeping fit and healthy. Many food stores and restaurants have sprouted up in Lowell, and from the crowds that eat in them during lunchtime, it seems these are popular eating places, patronized by the local population. A food business cannot survive without popular support. I was also informed by a woman who participated in this study that Khmer is now included as an international language in the school curriculum at the high school in Lowell. Golap, whom I interviewed for this study, indicated that she sent her children to a charter school in Lowell where the Khmer language is taught. These are definite signs of introduction of cultural diversity in a city that has been known for its immigrant history.

The Water Festival

Lowell has been the venue for an important annual cultural event, particularly so for Cambodia and Cambodians. Holding this event is a very significant achievement of the Cambodian community in Lowell. This is the Water Festival that was first hosted by the CMAA in partnership with University of Massachusetts in Lowell. Indeed, hosting this event was a factor in earning Lowell the title of All-American City in 1999.[36] The Water Festival is held in the month of August each year. It is fashioned after the annual boat race, held in Phnom Penh, Cambodia where the Mekong River converges with another river. The race begins in front of the royal palace and is the biggest festival of the country there. The boat race is held in November after the harvest season and is akin to giving thanks for a successful rice harvest, a staple for people of that region. Traditionally, the boat race is in celebration of water that is seen as integral and indispensable for sustaining life. Water is considered essential for various aspects of life—agriculture, economic prosperity, and spirituality—all things that people depend upon in life. According to Buddhist scripture, "the water festival is held to thank the spirit of the water, to pray for evil spirits to go away, and to honor the Dragon king who dwells in the water."[37] The boat race is like a big fair where people of all walks of life and ages gather from different regions to see and cheer the boat race and for those who participate in the race, possibly also to take the winner's trophy home with them. The Water Festival in Lowell is the largest Cambodian festival held outside of Cambodia. As many as 40,000 people attended the festival in 2004, and there were seventy-four vendors selling different items of Cambodian culture from food to arts and crafts, as well as dance and entertainment.[38] The Lowell Water Festival is the only one of its kind in the U.S. Many Cambodians feel that while they are not able to go to their country of origin, they can nevertheless experience its culture through events such as the Water Festival.

The Water Festival was the product of a dream to bring Cambodian culture to American people.[39] The Merrimack River (water) with its associated falls that was harnessed for energy purposes in Lowell was crucial for its economic prosperity as a factory town in the 19th century. The importance of this river in the history of Lowell made this festival that celebrated water as a source of life significant and symbolically important both for the old and the new residents of Lowell. The Mekong River and the Merrimack River were both important for economic prosperity and sustenance of life in these two disparate regions, and therefore adoption of this festival so many thousand miles removed from its original source in a different culture milieu seemed to be a natural fit. Initially, the Water Festival was conceived as an environmental program to educate the refugees about safety issues of consuming water and fish from the river, which was polluted.[40] It later blossomed into a big cultural event, drawing not only members of the community but also others from around the region that came to witness this huge show. The Water Festival was originally made possible with efforts of the CMAA in partnership with the University of Massachusetts Lowell's Center for Family, Work, and Community. It is now established as a separate nonprofit organization under the name of The Lowell Southeast Asian Water Festival, Inc. Its mission is to promote mutual harmony and understanding among Asian Americans and others through arts and cultural festivals and help in the preservation and protection of the cultural heritage of the Asian Americans of Greater Lowell area.

Angkor Dance Troupe

Another cultural organization formed in 1986 for the preservation of art and culture of Cambodia is the Angkor Dance Troupe of Lowell. Tim Chan Thou, one of the founders of this Dance Troupe, learned this art form in the refugee camps of Thailand before he migrated to the United States in 1982. His grandmother was a member of the Royal Dance Troupe that had visited the U.S. in the 1980s. That group no longer exists. Most of the traditional dancers of this art form had been killed under the brutal regime of Pol Pot and his followers. The dances were first revived in the refugee camps of Thailand to prevent their complete disappearance and to keep the tradition alive. Later, with the settlement of the refugees and immigrants into a viable Cambodian community in Lowell, this art form got a new breath of life with the formation of the Angkor Dance Troupe. Originally, it included a group of young dancers who came to Lowell from the refugee camps in Thailand. Their mission was to preserve Cambodian tradition and culture. The troupe, housed in the Mogan Cultural Center in Lowell, conducts its dancing lessons there. Classes are free of charge. There are more than seventy members ranging in ages from 5 to 25 years old participating in the troupe. Since its inception, this group has performed locally and nationally and is the only Cambodian dance group outside of Cambodia. The presence of this group in Lowell and its cultural contribution to the city was an additional factor that helped the city win the title of All-America City in 1999.[41]

Angkor Dance is performed in both classical and folk styles. The classical dance form was performed before the royal court. The folk dances were representative of the everyday rural life associated with activities of rice harvesting and other household chores of rural life. Both styles are integral part of traditional Cambodian performing art. This art form is tied to the very essence and identity of the Khmer people and resurrection of this dance form on U.S. soil is a way to maintain and perpetuate this identity that experienced severe destruction under Pol Pot's rule. Tim Chan Thou feels that by learning and performing this dance, children who are growing up in the U.S. will get to understand and appreciate Cambodian culture. He hopes that as the young initiates learn and master the tradition, they will be the teachers for children of tomorrow and in so doing the tradition will remain alive and well. But there is another socially necessary function that the Dance Troupe is performing for its young members. Induction into this cultural art form is also a very productive method of teaching the young ones of the richness of their cultural heritage and keeping kids out of the streets and gangs. By funneling energy into creative forms of artistic expression, the children of refugees are getting opportunities for using and discovering their artistic talent that they may have never otherwise gotten. But more importantly for many children, this has meant freedom from street life of gangs and violence. One young dancer has claimed that "Angkor Dance troupe is important to me because it keeps me out of trouble and helps me to keep on holding onto my schoolwork."[42] The Angkor Dance Troupe, in collaboration with the Lowell Police Department and Big Brothers/Big Sisters of Lowell, has sponsored youth programs to steer young people away from gangs by encouraging their involvement with Cambodian Dance.[43] In a retreat conducted by the Big Brothers/Big Sisters of Lowell, many young people were asked about factors that help them resist some of the temptations of street life. They indicated that involvement with Cambodian Dance Troupe helped them be proud of their cultural heritage, provided them with mentors and guides as role models, and gave them safe places to "hang out" with friends while they also enjoyed and had fun participating in dances. I was also told by one of the co-founders of the Troupe that modern dance forms such as hip hop and break dance have also been blended with traditional Cambodian styles to create new syncretic styles representing both the Cambodian and the American art forms.[44] The Monkey Dance is a product of such fusion and was performed at the White House in 1999 at the invitation of Hillary Clinton, when she was the First Lady. Some of the teenagers in this dance production are now in college pursuing academic careers. "Cambodian dance plays an important role for these young people, most of whom are the children of refugees, and goes beyond the actual dance techniques learned to enrich many aspects of their life: social, cultural, artistic and academic."[45]

Children and adults who perform this art form before audiences are emissaries of their traditional culture to others. While representing their art to the larger society, they are also contributing to the richness of the society that they are a part of. For many who have witnessed and been part of the trauma accompanying life of a refugee, being a part of the dance group can also be therapeutic and can lead to the healing of "fractured identities" and deep wounds. The troupe has entered into partnership with other social service providers in Lowell to help nurture young ones to aspire and prepare for colleges and be responsible citizens of the state.

Cambodian New Year Celebration

The New Year Festival was first celebrated in 1994. I attended the celebration once at the J.F.K. Plaza near the Lowell City Hall where the mayor of Lowell addressed the crowds attending the function. The New Year is the most important cultural event in the life of Khmer people. It is their biggest holiday. The Cambodian New Year is in April and is celebrated between April 13 and 15 in Cambodia. In Lowell it is celebrated on a weekend, because people cannot take time off from work during the day. People go to the temple, pray for prosperity for the coming year, and offer food to the monks. Some changes have been made to the celebrations here due to seasonal difficulties. April marks the beginning of summer in Cambodia. The crops have been harvested and stored away. People can relax and enjoy themselves. However, in the United States it is still very cold. Therefore, some of the traditional games where water is splashed on each other by young men and women as adults watch them are not possible here.[46] When I attended the festival, I kept thinking how cold the young boys and girls must have been feeling while dressed in their costumes for the dance that they performed in the plaza. It was a cold Saturday morning. Still, the fact that they are able to observe their cultural tradition so important in their lives so far away from their native land brings happy memories of the past. This is reflected in the comment made by Pere Pen, an Executive Director of CMAA, who noted, "It's kind of nostalgic for people who used to live in Cambodia."[47]

The above examples illustrate the efforts of the community leaders who came as refugees to this state approximately twenty years ago to help the community overcome some of the hardships encountered in settling in a new environment. The efforts and energies expended to implant homeland cultural traditions into the country of domicile have been intended to give children and adults a sense of identity and pride that is empowering and can help tackle the problems of despair and hopelessness that many refugees have succumbed to. These have also contributed to the richness of the culture of the city and its citizens.

However, these efforts do not mean that the process of settlement has been successfully accomplished and completed. There are problems of youth disenchantment leading to gang violence, the isolation of those who are linguistically handicapped, and in general the issues associated with economic disadvantages. A lot remains to be done to address the needs of large numbers of people who are not "making it." The average income level of Cambodians is still low. Compared to the Indians and Vietnamese, the other two Asian groups for which data on income is reported in the 2000 census, Cambodians have the lowest per capita and median income. Their per capita income is $9,727 (see Figure 4). Compared to the other Asian groups in Lowell they have the highest poverty rate (shown in Figure 5). Nearly one-quarter of Cambodian families live in poverty, which is 50% higher than the proportion in the general population.[48] Similarly, more than 38% of Cambodians over 25 years old have less than a ninth-grade education. Low educational levels are particularly acute among Cambodian females.[49] Large numbers of people—women and their families—without adequate language and market skills are struggling to survive. Children are growing up in families in an environment of despair and helplessness who need to be given hope and opportunities for better lives such that they refrain from joining groups that land them into trouble. Many families are culturally and economically unprepared to deal with the family problems they face and need resources to help them cope. The traumas experienced by these refugees further complicate their situations. These problems require education, training, and healing; only then can these be satisfactorily addressed. Some of the women in my study who have successfully been integrated into adult roles have had the benefit of education. They have also been blessed with family

110 | Between Two Cultures

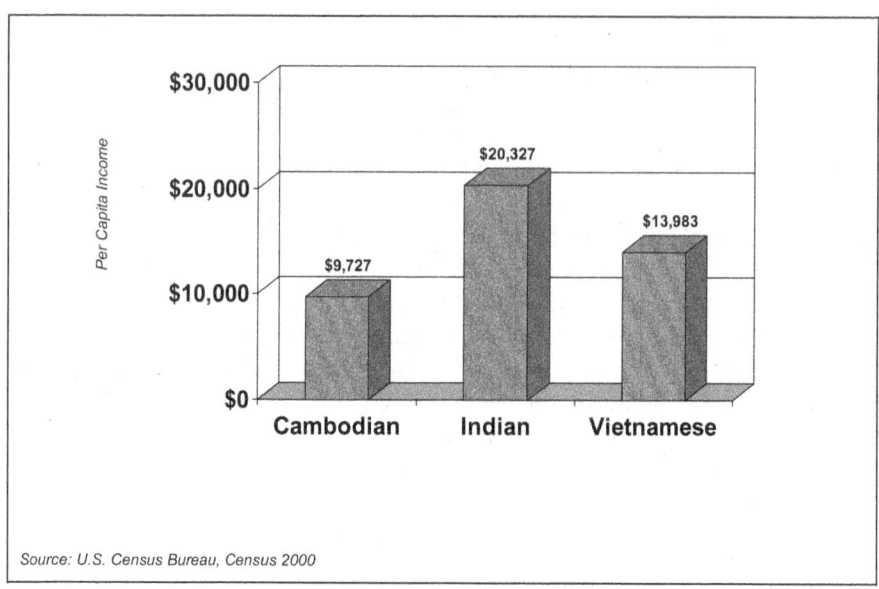

Figure 4. Per Capita Income by Asian Subgroup in Lowell

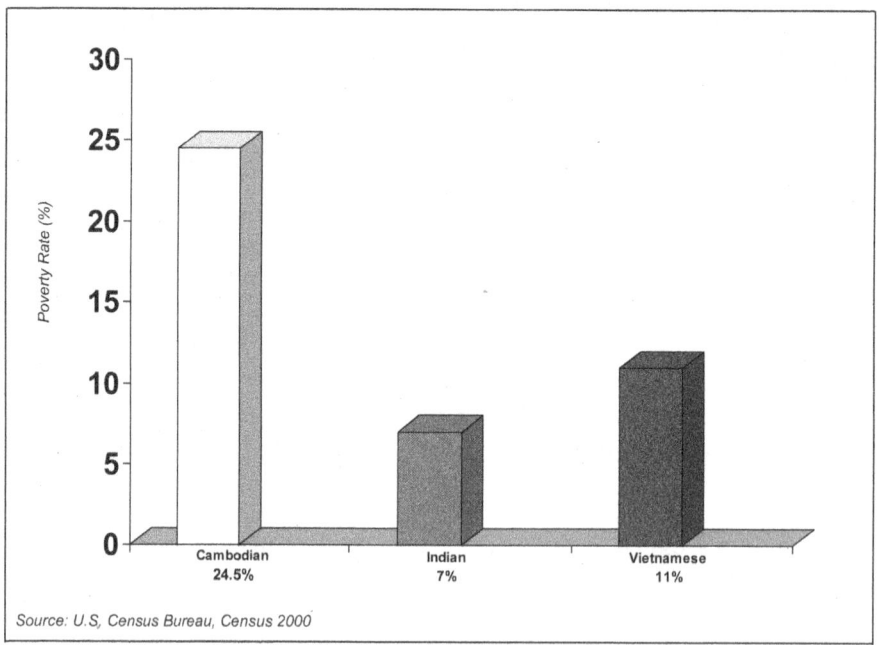

Figure 5. Poverty Rate by Asian Subgroup in Lowell

and community support. There are many Cambodians in Lowell in different professions and fields such as education, health, art, social services, and law enforcement. In my study the ones who were able to achieve success in life are those who had the opportunity of education. Education seems to play a pivotal role in accessing opportunities that can ensure a decent lifestyle and living. The importance of education and English language competency in enhancing one's economic prospects is documented in variety of sources. It plays a key role in ensuring a decent, safe, and comfortable quality of life, which is the reason why many came to the United States in the first place.

 CHAPTER SEVEN

Conclusion

In the past several decades the Asian population in this country has grown in numbers and in diversity. There are people from different regions of Asia that have settled in the United States for different reasons. Asian immigration got a boost when the Immigration and Naturalization Act was passed in 1965. Before then it was mainly people from the Far East such as China and Japan that represented the Asians in the United States. With the passage of the 1965 Act, Asians from many different regions came to settle in the United States. But these did not include Southeast Asians. The Cambodians started to arrive in sizable numbers after 1980 with the passage of the Refugee Act of 1980. This Act was in response to the large numbers of Cambodians trekking into neighboring Thailand and other countries to escape the terror and violence in their native land.

Cambodian refugees are different from many Asians who came voluntarily to this country before them, in pursuit of opportunities that they thought would be easier to realize here than if they had remained in their home countries. This difference has been in some ways important in their resettlement in this country. For one, as refugees they have been entitled to public assistance from the federal and state governments of their domiciles. Second, because their migration was involuntary in the sense that they came here to escape the "killing fields," they were unprepared for the culture and challenges of this society. So while they received help in resettlement, they lacked many of the credentials and traits that would allow them to fit in without challenges. Third, there were large numbers of women with children who came in as refugees because their husbands had been victims of the atrocities of the Pol Pot regime. Their adaptation into the mosaic of American culture and society thus provides us interesting insights into the process by which new ethnic groups, especially women, assimilate into the American way of life.

Social scientists studying immigrants coming into the United States have been concerned with the nature of adjustments they make as they adapt to life in this country. The process of integrating ethnically heterogeneous people into a single unified nation despite the diversity has been described by various terms such as assimilation, amalgamation, and cultural pluralism.[1] *Assimilation* stresses conformity to the dominant cultural model of American society. At a time when America was a young nation, the leaders of this country were concerned with keeping intact the distinctive identity that marked the American way. Newcomers had to be Americanized by giving up native traits and adopting those of the dominant group here. As peoples from different regions of the world, principally of European background, entered and settled in the U.S. as immigrants, the idea of *amalgamation* became accepted. The term "melting pot" best expressed this idea. America was heralded as a cultural melting pot where each new group, through its contribution to the existing society, was creating a new cultural synthesis that defined the distinctive nature of American society. The emphasis here was on fusion of different cultural ways into the U.S. cooking pot. *Cultural pluralism*, the third category of adjustment, recognizes the strength and value in diversity. Mutual reciprocity, giving and taking, and respect for different cultures were emphasized in this viewpoint. Liberty and equality were stressed, but this was not extended to all ethnic groups within the borders of the United States. Cultural pluralism was directed to European immigrants. It did not include non-English subcultures.[2]

American immigration did not include non-white peoples from countries of Asia and Africa until the middle of the 20th century. That happened only after the 1960s and brought the idea of multiculturalism, acknowledging the presence of non-white ethnic minorities in American society. It is interesting to note that these ideas and discourse about the nature of adjustment and integration of immigrants into mainstream American society correspond to the growth and increase in diversity of immigrants. The historical times and trends embedded therein, are reflected in this discourse. Thus the assimilation model of conformity to White Anglo-Saxon Americans emerged at a time when the hegemony of Western colonial power was entrenched throughout the world. It is unlikely to be accepted in an age of globalism where transnational migration has become accepted as people follow their agendas of personal goals and fulfillment across nations, making cultural boundaries between countries more fluid and tenuous.

The recognition and acknowledgment of ethnic diversity of the population within the country does not necessarily ensure a smooth and problem-free adaptation of such groups in the United States. "Making it in America" is also multifaceted with different forces contributing to it. First, political and economic situations may affect the reception of new residents into this country. The Act of 1965, which allowed and subsequently changed the ethnic composition of immigrants entering this country, was passed in an era when the U.S. was experiencing rapid social change with the demand for civil rights for people of color. The U.S. could not continue with business as usual at home and abroad. The mass exodus of refugees from Cambodia into neighboring Thailand following political turmoil in that country drew international attention. Thailand pressured the U.S. into finding a solution to the refugee problem since they were believed to have created it in the first place. The solution came by way of the Refugee Act of 1980 permitting large numbers of Cambodian and other refugees from that region to come to the U.S. The national guilt over the Vietnam War and the havoc created in its aftermath made many here at home sympathetic to acceptance of refugees from that region. From 1975 to 1992 approximately 150,000 Cambodians came to this country as refugees. The maximum numbers (approximately 90,000) arrived between 1980 and 1985. The United States took the largest numbers, although some went to other Western countries such as France or Australia. Initially, government policies and programs were formulated to place refugees in communities in the absence of relatives or friends who could sponsor them. However, soon communities of settlements through secondary migrations emerged as people learned of places where their kith and kin were concentrated. Although Cambodians are dispersed in many states across the nation, there are some regions with high concentrations. Lowell is the home to the largest Cambodian community in Massachusetts. The Cambodian Diaspora in Lowell, Massachusetts, is the second largest in the United States after Long Beach, California.

Second, the needs of the labor market also determine the reception given to the newcomers. In times of economic development and accompanying labor shortage, people have been encouraged to come to the U.S. Similarly, when there is a downturn in the economy, minority residents of color may find themselves in a particularly vulnerable position and be blamed for taking jobs away from others. Preexisting groups and individuals are likely to be hostile to new groups under such conditions, especially if they are seen as competitors to their jobs. If one examines the immigrant history of the U.S., one is likely to find numerous examples that illustrate the above. The Chinese in the third quarter of the nineteenth century were singled out for discriminatory treatment when the Unied States slid into a nationwide depression. Nowhere was this more visible than the state of California where the Chinese were concentrated in large numbers.[3] As the hostility against the Chinese mounted, different measures were taken that curtailed their freedoms, the ultimate of which was the Chinese Exclusion Act of 1882, which severely restricted their immigration into this country. More recently Helen Zia, a Chinese American, the author of *Asian American Dreams*, wrote about personally being rebuked by a person of European descent who told her to "Go back where you came from," and another white man who shouted at her, "hurry up, you Asian bitch."[4] These abuses were hurled at her when New York was experiencing a recession after the 1987 stock market crash and people's purses were affected. It was also a time when the immigrant population in the city had increased greatly, making them visible as a target responsible for the city's economic woes. This differential treatment is not restricted to the Chinese alone. In the twentieth century other minority groups also have been blamed for America's economic woes and subjected to hostility. When the Cambodian were beginning to come to Lowell as refugees and were assisted by the state in their rehabilitation, some students in my classes expressed their strong opposition to their presence in Lowell. They argued against the "dole" being handed to the refugees when they (the students) had to struggle and pay for everything themselves. It is ironic that most of these students were grand- or great-grandchildren of immigrants who had themselves experienced hostility when they had come to Lowell in pursuit of economic opportunities several generations ago.

The settlement of Cambodians in Lowell was aided by both political and economic factors. The governor of Massachusetts at that time and his wife were supportive of refugees and instructed the provision of state funds to help them resettle. At the time the Cambodian refugees arrived in Lowell, there were also some industries that were able to employ them at entry level jobs, which was a factor that pulled them into the state. As the population increased, many found work in shops and businesses opened by their compatriots.

The academic qualifications or absence of them also determine the outcome of adaptation of an incoming group. By and large people with skills that the market needs are likely to be in demand. Those lacking skills essential for economic survival also are likely to be socially disadvantaged. The 1990 census reported the high-income households among Asians were represented in the top educational and occupational categories. Similarly 2000 census data reports high levels of educational attainments among people of Asian origin although there is much diversity due to regional heritage.[5] The Asians with low incomes and high poverty rates were principally of Southeast Asian origins. As a group Cambodians can be distinguished from other Asians in terms of their educational and income backgrounds. The median family income of Cambodians according to the 1990 US Bureau of Census was approximately $18,000 annually with roughly 43% living below the poverty level. The 2000 census reports the Cambodian median income to be around $36,000 nationally. In Lowell, according to the 2000 census, Cambodians have the highest rate of poverty of all Asian residents in the city. According to the 1990 Census, more than 40% of the Cambodian population lacked education beyond the fifth grade and a majority of them did not have a workable knowledge of English. The same census figures reported that 70% of the people could not speak English 'very well' and 40% were linguistically isolated. The 2000 census data of Cambodians in Lowell also confirms the large numbers of Cambodians who are linguistically isolated and report that they speak English 'not very well.' This is confirmed from the small group of people that I have interviewed in my study. Indeed many of the older women were not even literate in Khmer, their native language. These statistics are cited to emphasize the importance of factors relevant in the process of adaptation of Cambodians in the U.S. The positive role of education in economic adaptation had been noted elsewhere.[6]

As the Cambodians settled in Lowell they faced a combination of opportunities and challenges mixed together. Everyone I spoke to reported being happy to come to the U.S. The freedom from violence and terror and the ability to lead normal and peaceful lives was greatly appreciated. Indeed, most of them did not want to return to their native land except for visiting relatives and friends left behind. In one particular case, a woman professionally a nurse in Cambodia was separated from her husband when the Pol Pot soldiers ordered everyone to vacate Phnom Penh. She did not have the chance to go back home to meet her husband. Years later she met him in the U.S. He wanted to return to Cambodia when the situation had stabilized. She refused to go back and instead remained here with her daughter who was in college at the time I interviewed her. After having sustained the trauma of separation and hardships in the refugee camps, she was thinking about her daughter and the opportunities she would have here. There was sadness in her speech, yet she chose to remain with her daughter who she thought would have better opportunities in the U.S. than in Cambodia. Her husband returned to Cambodia with another woman he had found. Almost all the women I spoke to mentioned the opportunities of personal freedom as one of the things most desirable of being here in the U.S. "You can do what you want to" was a common theme repeatedly heard. Yet this freedom was also a double-edged sword.

Many women with children were unhappy that they lacked control over their children because of the freedoms and rights children had available to them. These women thought that American society was too permissive and lenient in child-rearing methods where physical punishment in the form of hitting was frowned upon as abuse. Beating children for disobeying was an accepted practice in Cambodia. Obedience to elders was valued, and children were taught to follow the rules foisted upon them by their elders. Compliance could be enforced through physical punishment. Teachers and monks in charge of novices left in their care could resort to this method of disciplining in situations that demanded it. But such physical discipline could get them into trouble with the authorities responsible for overseeing children's rights and welfare in this country.[7] I heard one instance where a girl was so severely beaten that she sustained a fracture in her leg. This was the punishment meted to her to discourage her from having a boyfriend. Of course her fracture was explained as due to a fall. Many parents concerned with the dangers of freedom are very strict with their children, monitoring their behavior, not allowing them time to spend with friends after school. A young woman who was in college pursuing a bachelor's degree in the social sciences told me that she never went for sleepover parties to a friend's house. She was twenty-two years old when I first met her. Even so her mother strictly supervised her after college hours. She accepted her mother's discipline but her younger sister, whom I spoke to when I visited them in their house was unhappy that she could not do the things that her peers had the liberty to do such as going to the mall with friends. Her mother kept a strict watch over all the children to protect them from the attractions that adolescents succumb to. Her efforts paid off because all her children graduated from college, the eldest having completed her Ph.D. This family is an example of a success story despite the tension that children experienced being controlled by an all-powerful mother who was supported by her husband.

But many parents have not been as fortunate. Many women have been burdened with the dual responsibilities of economically providing for their families and also taking care of their children. Working long hours to meet their economic needs means leaving their children home alone unsupervised. Many of these women lacked the language competency to interface with people who were service providers. With little or no education they could not track the educational performance of their children. The helplessness and despair in families that struggled to survive made children of such families easy targets for groups who were on the watch to recruit new members in their gangs. A woman associated with the Light of Cambodia project attempted to enrich the lives of children by getting them interested in art and culture as a way to avoid gangs. She was telling me that gang leaders posted people outside schools to keep a watch on kids who could be easily recruited into antisocial activities. The children who were easy targets were those who sought to find support and love outside the home because of their inability to get it at home. Time and again I heard women speak of two things that they wanted their children to avoid. For girls it was premarital sex and for boys it was induction into gangs. Some parents, to prevent these problems, took a pre-emptive strike by marrying off their children before they could contract relations for themselves. Some very bright girls did not get to pursue an education as a result. Some became parents prematurely, when they were still children.

A large number of the refugees in Lowell came from very rural backgrounds with little formal education and knowledge of English language. This handicapped them. For those who were not young this was problematic. A middle-aged couple with five children who could not speak English seemed to be troubled by the future that they faced. How could they find jobs with which to earn incomes? was a question that plagued them. Language deficiency also affected their ability to parent and keep abreast of developments and events that they needed to be informed about. I recall when I visited them their eldest daughter who was in high school at the time was in the house. She appeared to be very angry and hostile toward her parents. As children enter schools, learn English and the American cultural rules of acting and behavior, the chasm that separates them from their parents grows. As they become the spokesperson for their families with the rest of the society, the power equation in the family changes with children becoming the power wielders. Not only does this sometimes lead them into problems within and outside the family, it also forces them to grow up and prevents them from being children.

The public assistance that refugees received upon arrival for resettlement was temporary. The community leaders involved with the CMAA reported that grants had been reduced with time. The goal of resettlement was to make refugees self-sufficient. The families that I interviewed received public assistance at one time or another. Some had successfully gotten off it as they became economically solvent. But for many others, getting off public welfare was like losing the safety net. Many women were afflicted with ailments that kept them dependent on public assistance. A woman I met had impaired vision that prevented her from working. Her husband likewise had a condition that prevented him from working. Both of these individuals suffered bodily injury due to their experiences in the refugee camps. They could not work and the possibility of not getting any assistance was frightening. One community activist told me of the incidence of psychosomatic blindness that afflicted many older refugees. Her mother was one of them. Among the refugees with traumatic experiences due to violence and war that dictated their exit from their home countries, the group that was worst off were the Cambodians. It was their exposure to violence and death, and loss of family members that was a predictor of their psychological health. After being here for some years, its effect receded to be replaced by anxiety over unemployment or economic vulnerability. This has been documented.[8]

As children of refugees enter schools and begin their participation in the school system, they also learn cultural norms that are at odds with traditional norms advocated and subscribed by their parents. One of the issues that magnifies this divide occurs when children come of age and have to make choices about choosing their partners. This is an issue that has received a lot of attention. There have been parenting classes organized by the CMAA to help parents and children adjust to their environment here. My own research indicates how difficult it is to insulate children from the forces of the larger mainstream society. Of course, different solutions are adopted to deal with this issue as children come of age. Some women arrange the marriage of their daughters while they are still in their teens to prevent them from engaging in "undesirable" behaviors. Other children chose their partners themselves but maintain a façade of tradition by observing the rituals and customs associated with tying the knot. There were still others who go against tradition by openly defying their parents' wishes. Finally, there were those who totally abandon tradition by adopting a course of action that would not be acceptable or likely to happen in Cambodia. The fourth category includes the group of woman who live with their partners before officially marrying them. Some of them also have children premaritally. In fact, a woman who worked in a service provider role to young

Cambodian parents stated that as adolescents enter school "cultural stuff goes out the window." In schools they are exposed to a new and different world where 'sex is okay, not a big deal.' Many teenagers use their body as a source of power to rebel. Others are misinformed about their bodies. This same service provider also observed middle-class girls or girls who are well anchored to the groups they belong to and have college educational aspirations are not sexually active compared to girls of lesser economic standing. My sense is that the younger generation of Cambodian girls and boys increasingly accept the American rules of meeting and going out with friends on dates. Adolescents or young adults view sex mixing differently from the way their parents schooled in the old traditions see it. This modern and global trend transcends societies around the world with "traditional" family form with emphasis on arrangement of matches giving way to a "modern" more democratic family type where freedom of choice is the mark of equality and liberty. This freedom and equality embedded in modern relationships is an anathema to parents raised in traditional families, who therefore resist it. Modern family relations are democratic and challenge the traditional structures of power, as the goals of family and couple relationship change from catering to the needs of the group to those of personal fulfillment of the partners.

Thus far the above discussion emphasizes the ways in which this incoming group into the U.S. is affected and accommodates to the host society. It is true that the newcomers have to "fit in" and accept the cultural rules and laws of the society they are settling into. But by their entry they also introduce and initiate changes into the host society. Lowell in the last twenty years has changed remarkably with infusion of cultural traits associated with the Cambodian people. There are various ethnic restaurants where Southeast Asian cuisine is served and these are crowded during lunch hours. Most of the people going there to eat are not Cambodians. This is a significant departure from when I started my professional life in Lowell three decades ago. One could not eat in restaurants if one did not eat beef and/or was a vegetarian. There are innumerable Southeast Asian shops and businesses that have opened, pumping life into the economy. Lowell earned the title of All America City because of its cultural contribution to the life of the city. The boat race or the Water Festival in Lowell is the largest Cambodian cultural event, outside of Phnom Penh in Cambodia. It has become an annual cultural event drawing more visitors to the city than the traditional folk festivals organized by the National Park. The Angkor Dance Troupe, founded to keep traditional Cambodian dance forms alive has brought cultural and performing art traditions from Cambodia into America that is being used to empower a generation of children of refugees who can learn and personally feel the glorious heritage of their country through its dances. These dances also have a positive community-building role. Through its medium kids are kept off destructive and antisocial behavior while contributing to the cultural life of the city. In a documentary of the Dance Troupe,[9] the principal dancers honestly share their life stories about how the dances were a turning point in their lives from a potential life on the street to a life of college education that will enable them to realize the American dream. As a Cambodian community leader suggested, that as a people "we are not just taking from the city" but are also are contributing to its life. The Buddhist temples that were established in the 1980s added a new dimension to the religious diversity of the city. Before the advent of the Southeast Asians into Lowell the churches were principally of Christian denominations. Buddhist temples and their monks played a role in the process of settlement by allowing those who believed in the faith to be Cambodian while in America. In fact, their role extended beyond maintenance of faith of its members. Religion was used in partnership with other law enforcement groups to bring hope and betterment in the lives of troubled children who were victims of the war and violence that their parents had lived through.

Cambodians, like other groups that have come into a Lowell before them, are leaving an imprint in the ethnic history of the city. Their sheer numerical strength gives them a base to operate from such that their needs can only be ignored at the risk of compromising the peace and health of the larger society. As the refugees and their children get the skills and tools to function in the society that they now believe themselves to be part of, they will be able to be self-sufficient and make contributions to the communities that they live in. The dividends that will accrue will be greater than the costs incurred in their settlement. The cultural journeys were embarked upon by the women in this study when the decision was made to seek refuge in the U.S. and start anew. These journeys were part of the process that many immigrants before them have undertaken. In some ways their experiences are not unique. Many Asian immigrants have experienced the dilemma of being torn between the "old" and "new" particularly when their children enter adolescence and later are on the verge of entering adulthood. This is best reflected in family dynamics of interpersonal relationships involved in selection of a life partner. In other ways their stories are unique. The political events at home determined and in many ways forced their chances and choice of making it in America. One needs to recall that a lot of the refugees were women who came here without husbands who were entrusted with the responsibility of taking care of themselves and their dependent children. After the initial period of euphoria was over, there were problems of survival that had to be addressed. There were structural and cultural issues that needed attention. The coping strategies that are worked out involve the larger institutions and groups whose resources have to be creatively utilized in the service of the Cambodian community. Both the refugees and the receiving society are mutually interdependent in the outcome of the settlement process that affects both of them. And this has to be kept in mind by those who are engaged in policymaking and programs of empowerment so that the 'host' country does indeed become the "home" country.

Notes

◨ CHAPTER ONE

1. Portes, Alejandro, & Rumbaut, Ruben G. *Immigrant America: A Portrait*, University of California Press, 1996, p. 10.
2. Aikman, D., & Jackson, D. "Not So Welcome Anymore," *Time*, Fall 1993, p. 10.
3. Elson, John. "The Great Migration," *Time*, Fall 1993, p. 28.
4. Handlin, Oscar. *The Uprooted: The Epic Story of the Great Migrations That Made the American People*, Little Brown and Company, 1973, p. 3.
5. Dudley, William (Ed). *Immigration: Opposing Viewpoints*, Greenhaven Press, 1990, p. 13.
6. Daniel, Roger. *Coming to America: A History of Immigration and Ethnicity in American Life*, Harper Perennial, 1991, p. 276.
7. Blewett, Peter F. "The New People: An Introduction to the Ethnic History of Lowell," in *Cotton Was King*, edited by Arthur L. Eno, New Hampshire Publishing House, 1976, p. 191.
8. Barrett, James R., & Roediger, David. "How White People Became White" in *White Privilege*, edited by Paula S. Rothenberg, Worth Publishers, 2002, p. 29.
9. Cited by Zia, Helen. *Asian American Dreams*, Farrar, Strauss and Giroux, 2000, p. 52. The *Boston Globe* also reported a spate of violence against Asian Americans in Boston in an article published in the newspaper by Gregory Witcher under the title "Tattered Dreams," March 31, 1986.
10. Quoted in The *Boston Globe*, December 31, 1984.
11. The distinction between immigrants and refugees has to do with their legal status of entry into this country that determines whether the person is entitled for federal assistance. For the purpose of this study, refugees are considered a class of immigrants who share similar experiences common to members of their ethnic group.
12. Daniel, *op.cit.* p. 238.

13. Statistical Abstract of the United States, 82nd ed. U.S. Bureau of Census, 1961, p. 93.

14. Min, Pyong, G. "An Overview of Asian Americans," in *Asian Americans: Contemporary Trends and Issues*, edited by Pyong G. Min, Sage Publications, 1995, p. 11.

15. "Asian Population," U.S. Census Bureau, Census 2000, Summary File 1, Table 2

16. The term Asian includes people of different nationalities from the continent of Asia who differ from each other in many ways.

17. Ebihara, May M. "Khmer," in *Refugees in the United States: A Reference Handbook*, edited by David W. Haines, Greenwood, 1985, p. 134.

18. Rumbaut, Ruben G. "Vietnamese, Laotians and Cambodian Americans" in *Asian Americans*, edited by Pyong Gap Min, Sage Publications, 1995, p. 232.

19. Kitano, Harry H. L. & Daniels, Roger. *Asian Americans: Emerging Minorities*, Prentice Hall, 1988 p. 4.

20. *Times of India*, June 12, 2001, p. 12.

21. "The Foreign Born Population in the United States," U.S. Bureau of Census, Washington, DC., 1993.

22. Portes & Rumbaut, *op.cit.*, p. 84.

23. *Ibid.*, p. 26.

24. Kibria, Nazli. *Family Tight Rope: The Changing Lives of Vietnamese Americans*, Princeton University Press, 1993, p. 15.

25. Pailla. Felix, M. *Latino Ethnic Consciousness: The Case of Mexican Americans & Puerto Ricans*, University of Notre Dame Press, 1985, p. 23.

26. Early, Frances H. "The French Canadian Family Economy and the Standard of Living in Lowell, Massachusetts, 1870," in *The Continuing Revolution*, edited by Robert Weible, Lowell Historical Society, 1991, p. 237.

27. *Ibid.*

28. *The Lowell Sun*, February 16, 1989.

29. *Ibid.*

30. Portes & Rumbaut, *op.cit.*, p. 95.

31. Portes and Rumbaut, *op.cit.*, p. 100.

32. Kibria, *op.cit.*, p. 120.

33. *The Lowell Sun*, July 29, 1993.

34. Banister, J., & Johnson, P. "After the Nightmare: The Population of Cambodia," in *Genocide and Democracy in Cambodia: The Khmer Rouge, The United Nations and the International Community*, edited by Ben Kiernan, Yale University, 1993, p. 70.

35. Gerson, J. "The Cambodian Americans in Lowell, Massachusetts: A Cautionary Tale of New Immigrants and Refugee Political Incorporation," in *New Immigrants in New England*, edited by Hilary Silver & Jose Itzigsohn, University of Minnesota Press, 2006, (forthcoming).

36. Lessinger, J. *From the Ganges to the Hudson: Indian Immigrants in the New York City*, Allyn & Bacon, 1995, p. 36.

37. Dasgupta, Shamita D. "Marching to a Different Drummer? Sex Roles of Asian Indian Women in the United States," in *Women and Therapy*, Summer/Fall 1986, p. 298.

38. Many women expressed their concerns and difficulties in raising and controlling children in the United States. The occurrence of teenage pregnancy among

Cambodians has been reported in local newspapers as well in official sources. Hundreds of teen parents and advocates visited the State House in Boston to lobby for funds to support programs for teenage pregnancy prevention and getting teen parents back in educational tracks. *The Lowell Sun*, March 24, 2004.

39. Tizon, Alex. "Time and Distance Can't Bury Memories of the Killing Fields" in *The Seattle Times*, Vol. 4, Article 83, Jan. 23, 1994.

◻ CHAPTER TWO

1. Refer to Kamm, Henry. *Cambodia: Report From a Stricken Land*, Arcade Publishing, 1998 for an account of the events leading to the tragedy in Cambodia in which countries such as the United States, Vietnam, and Cambodia played roles.

2. Ung, Loung. *First They Killed My Father: A Daughter of Cambodia Remembers*, Harper Collins, 2000; Pran, Dith. *Children of Cambodia's Killing Fields*, Yale University Press, 1997.

3. Bankston, Carl L. "Cambodian Americans," in *The Gale Encyclopedia of Multicultural America*, edited by J. Galens, A. Sheets, & R. Young, Vol. 1, Gale Research, Inc., 1995, p. 224.

4. http://www.cia.gov/cia/publications/factbook

5. Ebihara, May M., et. al. *Cambodian Culture Since 1975*, Cornell University Press, 1994, p. 10.

6. http://www.cia.gov/cia/publications/factbook.

7. Welaratna, U. *Beyond the Killing Fields: Voices of Nine Cambodian Survivors*, Stanford University Press, 1993, p. 35.

8. Phim, Toni S., & Thompson, A. *Dance in Cambodia*, Oxford University Press, 1999, p. 4.

9. Rooney, D. *Angkor: An Introduction to the Temples*, Passport Books, 1997, p. 25.

10. Welratna, *op.cit.*, p. 13.

11. Becker, E. *When the War was Over*, Public Affairs, 1998, p. 35.

12. Welaratna, *op.cit.*, p. 15.

13. Chandler, D. *A History of Cambodia*, Westview Press, 1996, p. 2.

14. Ibid., p. 197.

15. Becker, *op.cit.*, p. 8.

16. Becker, *op.cit.*, p. 122.

17. Frieson, K. "Revolution and Rural Responses in Cambodia," in *Genocide and Democracy in Cambodia*, edited by B. Kiernan, Monograph Series 41, Yale University Southeast Asia Studies, 1993, p. 34.

18. Kamm, *op.cit.*, p. 117.

19. Becker, *op.cit.*, p. 160.

20. Pran, p. x.

21. Smith-Hefner, N. *Khmer American: Identity and Moral Education in a Diasporic Community*, University of California Press, 1999, p. 2.

22. Ung, *op.cit.*, p. 22.

23. Becker, *op.cit.*, p. 21.

24. Pran, *op.cit.*, p. xi.

25. Smith-Hefner, *op.cit.*, p. 2.

26. Gyallay-Prap, P. *Khmer Monk Education in the Thai Border Camps*, Amherst, 1990, p. 2.
27. Smith-Hefner, *op.cit.*, p. 7.
28. Reported in the *Lowell Sun*, July 3, 1994.
29. Ung, *op.cit.*, p. 31.

Chapter Three

1. The U.S. Commission on Immigration Reform held hearings in the Boot Mills on using Lowell as a national model for successful immigration, The *Lowell Sun*, July 29, 1994.
2. Karr, Ronald D, *New England at a Glance*, Branch Line Press, Pepperill: MA, 1993, p. 208.
3. Wilkie, R., & Tager, J. *The Historical Atlas of Massachusetts*, University of Massachusetts Press, 1991, p. 52.
4. Solomon, S. "Computer Boom Town," in *Science Digest*, 1983, p. 108.
5. Miller, M. "Who Won the War," in *The Continuing Revolution*, edited by Robert Wieble, Lowell Historical Society, 1991, p. 317.
6. *Refugees and Immigrants in Massachusetts: An Overview of Selected Communities*, Office of Refugee and Immigrant Health, Boston, Massachusetts, 1996.
7. The figures reported in The *Lowell Sun*, August 2, 1994 were taken from *USA Today*.
8. Chandler, D. *A History of Cambodia*, Westview Press, 1996, p. 314.
9. Becker, E. *When the War War Over*, Public Affairs, 1998, p. 453.
10. Mak, mentioned in the previous chapter, was sent back to Cambodia and had to walk through a narrow lane infested with land mines where any wrong step could have ended her life.
11. Russell, S. S. "Migration Patterns of U.S. Foreign Policy Interest," in *Threatened Peoples, Threatened Borders*, edited by Teitelbaum & Weiner, W. W. Norton, 1995, p. 74.
12. Zolberg, A. R. "From Invitation to Interdiction" in *Threatened Peoples and Threatened Borders*, *op.cit.*, p. 135.
13. Vialet, J. "U.S. Refugee Admissions and Resettlement Policy," *Migration World Magazine*, Vol. 28, Issue 1/2, January 1, 2000.
14. Daniels, R. *Coming to America: A History of Immigration & Ethnicity in American Life*, Harper Perrenial, 1991, p. 346.
15. Coleman, C. M. "Cambodians in the United States," in *The Cambodian Agony*, edited by D. Ablin & M. Hood, M. E. Sharpe, Inc., 1990, p. 371.
16. Coleman, *op.cit.*, p. 370.
17. Ung, *First They Killed My Father: A Daughter of Cambodia Remembers*, Yale University Press, 1997, p. 230.
18. The Asian Population 2000, US Department of Commerce Economics and Statistics Administration, US Census Bureau, February 2002.
19. U.S. Committee for Refugees, report December 1987.
20. Rumbaut, Ruben G. "Vietnamese, Laotians and Cambodian Americans," in *Asian Americans*, edited by Pyong Gap Min, Sage Publications, 1995, p. 240.

21. Pho, H. B "The Politics of Refugee Resettlement in Massachusetts," in *Migration World*, Vol, XIX, No. 4, 1991, p. 8.

22. *Ibid.*, p. 9

23. John Silver's stinging comment against the pro-refugee policy of the state in *The Boston Globe*, January 26, 1990.

24. Pyle, Jean L. "The Impact of Immigration Policy on Local Economies: The Importance of the Phenomena of Secondary Migration," Lowell, MA, 1994 (Unpublished paper).

25. Mortland, A. Carol, & Ledgerwood, Judy. "Secondary Migration Among Southeast Asian Refugees in the United States," *Urban Anthropology*, Vol. 16(3–4), 1987, p. 297.

26. A woman reporter who worked in the *Lowell Sun* revealed this to me.

27. Higgins, James, & Ross, Joan. *Fractured Identities: Cambodia's Children of War*, Loom Press, 1997, p. 14.

28. Portes, A. & Rumbaut, R. *Immigrant America: A Portrait*, University of California Press, 1996, p. 29.

29. Choldin, H. M. "Kinship Networks in the Migration Process" in *International Migration Review*, Vol. 7 # 2, 1973, pp. 163–175.

30. Mortland & Ledgerwood, *op.cit.*, p. 308.

31. Higgins & Ross, *op.cit.*, p. 15.

32. Chea, Phala, *Effects of Cultural and Ethnic Identity on Academic Performance and Self Esteem of Cambodian Adolescents*, Ph. D. thesis, Univesity of Massachusetts Lowell, 2003, p. 14.

33. Fenn, J. "Study: State Immigrant Count Booming" *The Lowell Sun*, June 20, 2005.

CHAPTER FOUR

1. "Social and Economic Characteristics," Mass 1990 Census of Population, U.S. Department of Commerce, Table 11.

2. U.S. Census Bureau, 2000, Summary File 3.

3. Dickson, Mary C. "Executive Summary: Asians and Pacific Islanders in America: A Demographic Profile," Population Resource Center, 2004.

4. Portes, A. & Rumbaut, R. *Immigrant America: A Portrait*, University of California Press, 1996, p. 7.

5. Rumbaut Ruben G., "Vietnamese, Laotians and Cambodian Americans" in *Asian Americans: Contemporary Trends and Issues*, Sage Publications, 1995, p. 233.

6. U.S Census 2000 Summary File 2.

7. Silka, L. "Addressing the Challenge of Community Collaboration," in *Approaches to Sustainable Development*, edited by Robert Forrant et al., University of Massachusetts Press, 2001, p. 361.

8. *The Lowell Sun*, May 16, 1993.

9. Pere Pen at the CMAA office spoke of the difficulties facing the Cambodian refugees who did not have the wherewithal to function in this society.

10. Welaratna, *Beyond the Killing Fields: Voices of Nine Cambodian Survivors*, Stanford University Press, 1993, p. 56.

11. Nien-Chu Kiang, P. "When Know-Nothings Speak English Only," in *The State of Asian America*, edited by Karin Aguilar-San Juan, South End Press, 1993, p. 131.

12. *Boston Sunday Herald,* September 4, 1988.

13. This was the sentiment expressed by many women I interviewed for this study.

14. Cambodians ask "Have you eaten rice?" as part of a greeting, comparable to asking how are you as a form of greeting in the U.S.

15. Ponchaud, Rev. F. "Approaches to the Khmer Mentality," Cambodian Apostolate, Pastoral Care of Migrants and Refugees, Washington, DC, unpublished paper.

16. Higgins, Kathleen, "Language Conflict in the Immigrant Population: Identity vs. Americanization," unpublished student paper, December 2001, p. 3.

17. Welaratna, p. 117.

18. Wilson, William, J. *When Work Disappears: The World of the New Urban Poor,* Vintage Books, 1997, p. 117.

19. 2003 Southeast Asia Resource Action Center, www.searac.org.

20. "Asian Americans in Lowell," U.S. Census, 2000.

21. "Southeast Asians" in *Refugees and Immigrants in Massachusetts: An Overview of Selected Communities,* Massachusetts Department of Public Health, 1999.

22. Leiper, Sochua Mu, "Reconstructing the Fabric of Women's Lives," in *Connexions,* Summer 1994.

23. Cambodian Times on the Net, Nov. 18–24, 1996.

24. U.S. Census, 2000.

25. In a Cambodian New Year celebration that I attended several years ago, the then Mayor of Lowell, who was the guest of honor at that event, congratulated the community for the academic performance of its children, many of whom were graduating as valedictorians in their classes.

26. The *Lowell Sun,* November 30, 1989.

27. Phone conversation with Phala Chea on June 8, 2005.

28. These problems are not limited to Cambodians alone.

29. Alvarez, L. "Interpreting New Worlds for Parents," *New York Times,* October 1, 1995.

30. Yang, K. Y. "Southeast Asian Americans and Higher Education," in *Evaluation of Asian Pacific Americans in Education,* www.searac.org.

31. This example is reported in the *Lowell Sun,* July 29, 1993.

32. "Learning from Diverse Voices: Seminar on Southeast Asian Refugees in the Mill City. Changing Families, Communities and Institutions," Lowell, Massachusetts, June 2, 2005.

33. Betty Bogs, involved with initial sponsorship and teaching English language classes to refugees, noted that young Cambodian girls miss out on several things that are part of normal growing up in America. She indicated instances she knew of where girls were married while they were still in their teens.

34. Um, Khatharya. "Resettlement into Limbo: Implication for the Schooling and Education of Cambodian Children," in *Unfamiliar Partners: Asian Parents and American Public Schools,* edited by Joan, et al., National Coalition of Advocates for Students, 1997, p. 35.

35. Tirella, R. "Growing up in America" *Lowell Sun,* July 29, 1993.

36. Saheli had organized workshops in Wellesley College in Wellesley, MA, to discuss and provide a forum to highlight some of the issues South Asian men and women experience due to cultural conflicts, February 12, 2005.

37. These problems are also seen in other ethnic communities in Lowell.

38. Pho, Lan T. "Cultural Behavior and Academic Performance among Southeast Asian Students in Lowell," paper presented at the Lowell History Roundtable, December 11, 1996.
39. Davis, Carolyn. "Cambodian Activist Updates Women's Status," www.cats.ohiou.edu.
40. Tenhula, John. *Voices From South East Asia*, Holmes & Meier, 1991, p. 180.
41. Rubin, L. *Families on the Fault Line*, Harper Perennial, 1994, p. 78.
42. Kibria, N., p. 181.

CHAPTER FIVE

1. I have been told by some of the women I interviewed that acting in ways deemed to be American is viewed negatively by their compatriots.
2. Vera T. Tith, *The Culture of Cambodia*, (Unpublished undated document).
3. Seidman, S. *Romantic Longings: Love in America, 1830–1980*, Routledge, 1919, p. 49.
4. Cited by Nancy Hefner in *Khmer American: Identity and Moral Education in a Diasporic Community*, University of California Press, 1999, p. 175.
5. Chang, Iris. *The Chinese in America: A Narrative History*, Viking, 2003, p. 193.
6. Goode, W. J., *World Revolutions and Family Patters*, Free Press, 1963, p. 2.
7. In an interview in 1995 Erika Hazard reported this. She worked in health providing service organization to young parents in Lowell.
8. Ledgerwood, J. "Gender Symbolism and Cultural Change," in *Cambodian Culture since 1975: Homeland and Exile*, edited by M. Ebihara, C. Mortland, & J. Ledgerwood, Cornell University Press, 1994, p. 125.
9. Many of these norms of morality Cambodian women learn from mythology and folklore. Some interesting stories are reported by Sophiline Cheamin, "An Honorable Life" (source unknown); Chey, Elizabeth. "The Status of Khmer Women," in *Cambodia: Beauty & Darkness*, 1995, www.members.aol.com/bsharp26/cambodia/woem.html.
10. Hefner, *op.cit.* Nancy. p. 175.
11. Goode, *op.cit.*, pp. 1–26.
12. Giddens, Anthony. *Runaway World*, Routledge, 2001, p. 81.
13. Hirschman, C. "Studying Immigrant Adaptation from the 1990 Population Census" in *The New Second Generation*, edited by Alejandro Portes, Russell Sage Foundation, 1996, p. 71.
14. Hefner, *op.cit.*, p. 177.
15. *Ibid.*
16. Marcucci, John. "Cultural Consumption: Cambodian Peasant Refugees and Television in the 'First World,'" in Ebihara et al., *Cambodian Culture Since 1975*, Cornell University Press, 1994, p. 142.

CHAPTER SIX

1. Pho, Hai B. "The Politics of Refugee Resettlement in Massachusetts," in *Migration World*, Vol. XIX, No. 4, 1991, p. 9.
2. The *Boston Globe*, August 1, 1985.
3. The *Boston Globe*, December 31, 1984.

4. Lam, M. Daniel. "How Massachusetts became a Refugee Friendly State," in *Not Just Victims*, edited by Sucheng Chan, University of Illinois Press, 2003, p. 112.

5. *Ibid.*, 120.

6. This was reported by Pere Pen the CMAA Executive Director that I interviewed in 1995.

7. Lam, *op.cit.*, p. 119.

8. The *Lowell Sun*, July 7, 1993.

9. Khoeun, Samkhann. "Lowell, Massachusetts, the 'Long Beach of the East Coast,'" in *Not Just Victims*, p. 144. Refer to Koeun for a discussion of CMAA initiatives.

10. Interview with Sophy Theam, involved with the program known as Light of Cambodian Children, August 2004.

11. Nancy Costello's report on Whiz Kids? Myth and Reality of Asian Students, The *Lowell Sun*, April 25, 1988.

12. An electronic message from Victoria Fahlberg indicated that according to an NCE report on Asians dropouts, the dropout rate for those who started high school in 1998 and did not complete it in 2000 is 50%. This can give an idea of what is happening to Cambodian students since they are the largest group of Asians enrolled in schools in Lowell.

13. *Boston Globe*, June 6, 1985.

14. Interview with Sophy Theam.

15. Khin, M. Aung, & Yu, N. "Educational Experiences and Demographics of Cambodians in Lowell, MA: Varying Interactions With and Treatment by Youth Serving Systems and Social Institutions" (working title), forthcoming.

16. Khoeun, *op.cit.*, pp. 144–145.

17. *Boston Globe*, July 19, 2004.

18. *Ibid.*

19. Interview with Vong Ros on September 1, 2004.

20. Refer to the website maintained by CALL.

21. Morris, A. *The Origin of the Civil Rights Movement*, The Free Press, 1984, pp. 4–5.

22. Nien-Chu Kiang, p. 135.

23. Mitchell, B. "Good Citizens at the Least Cost per Pound" in Wieble p. 125.

24. Welaratna, *Beyond the Killing Fields: Voices of Nine Cambodian Survivors*, Stanford University Press, 1993, p. 47.

25. *Ibid.*, p. 35.

26. "Rebuilding the Temple: Cambodians in America," National Endowment for the Humanities, 1991.

27. Sieng Sak, cited by Thompson, S. "Faith Based Approaches to Community Service and Civic Engagement" (unpublished paper), July 2004, p. 10.

28. Cohen, Gillian, quoted in Thompson, *op.cit.*, p. 8.

29. *New York Times*, July 26, 2003.

30. *Lowell Sun*, May 23, 2003.

31. *New York Times*, July 26, 2003.

32. *Lowell Sun*, May 23, 2003.

33. Interview with Sam Khan Khoeun, September 23, 2004.

34. Tooch Van, comment made at the seminar, "Learning from Different Voices," Lowell MA, June 2, 2005.

35. Smith-Hefner, Nancy J. "Rebuilding the Temple: Buddhism and Identity among Khmer Americans," in *Diasporic Identity: Selected Papers on Refugees and Immigrants*, edited by Carol A. Mortland, American Anthropological Association Committee on Refugees and Immigrants, 1998, p. 59.

36. This was disclosed to me in an interview I had with Sam Khan Khoeun, former Executive Director of CMAA and a community leader, who has attempted to introduce and educate both the native and Cambodian refugees and immigrants the richness of Cambodian heritage and culture.

37. "8th Annual Southeast Asian Water Festival, Saturday 21st August" www.lowellwaterfestival.com.

38. This was suggested by Chuck Sart, a community leader in Lowell who is also the current President of CMAA in an interview in September 2004.

39. This is the way Sam Kahn Khoeun described its inception in an interview I had with him. He was the Executive Director of CMAA originally involved with organizing this festival.

40. Sam Kahn Khoeun, mentioned above, revealed this.

41. Congressman Martin T. Meehan Press release July 20, 1999, www.house.gov/meehan/press.

42. Quoted by Thompson, S. T. "Angkor Dance Troupe," unpublished paper.

43. Wood, Hayley. "Julie Mallozzi's Monkey Dance," *Mass Humanities*, Fall 2001.

44. George Chigas indicated this in a conversation that I had with him in the fall of 2004.

45. Thomson, S. P. "Angkor Dance Troupe" (Unpublished paper).

46. The *Lowell Sun*, April 12, 1994.

47. Ibid.

48. "Asian Americans in Lowell," U.S. Census, 2000, Summary File 1.

49. Ibid.

CHAPTER SEVEN

1. Rose, Peter I. *They and We: Racial and Ethnic Relations in the United States*, McGraw-Hill, 1997, p. 80.

2. Appleton, N. *Cultural Pluralism in Education*, New York: Longman, 1993, p. 3.

3. Chang, Iris. *The Chinese American: A Narrative History*, Viking, 2003, p. 117.

4. Zia, Helen. *Asian American Dreams*, Farrar, Strauss & Giroux, 2000, p. 85.

5. U.S. Census Bureau, *Statistical Abstract of the United States: 2004–2005*.

6. Bach, R.L. & Carroll, Seguin, R. "Labor Force Participation, Household Composition and Sponsorship among Southeast Asian Refugees," in *International Migration Review*, 1986, 20(2), 381–404.

7. Massachusetts in 2005 has ruled against corporal punishment of children, making it illegal.

8. Rumbaut, R. "Vietnamese, Loatians & Cambodian Americans," in P. G. Min (ed.), *Asian Americans: Contemporary Trends & Issues*, Sage Publication, 1995, p. 260.

9. Refer to Mallozzi, J. *The Monkey Dance* (video).

Illustrations

Picture of torture under Khmer Rouge

134 | Illustrations

Scene from Rural Cambodia

Scene from Rural Cambodia

Khmer Children in Thai Refugee Camp

136 | Illustrations

Angkor Dance Troupe

Classical Dancers, Angkor Dance Troupe

Water Festival

Water Festival

American-Khmer wedding in Lowell. © James Higins

Cambodian Refugee family arriving in Logan Airport, Boston, MA. © James Higgins

Khmer student graduates from high school in Lowell. © James Higgins